Strong Rhythms and Rhymes

Language and Literacy Development Through Sentence Combining

Carol J. Strong, Ed.D. • William Strong, Ph.D.

Thinking Publications

Eau Claire, Wisconsin

09   08   07   06   05   04   03   02   10 9 8 7 6 5 4 3 2

Library of Congress Cataloging-in-Publication Data

Strong, Carol J.
    Strong rhythms and rhymes : language and literacy development through sentence combining / Carol J. Strong, William Strong.
        p. cm.
    Includes bibliographical references (p.) and indexes.
    ISBN 1-888222-32-8 (pbk.)
    1. Language arts (Elementary)—Problems, exercises, etc. 2. Children—Language. 3. English language—Phonology. 4. English language—Syntax. 5. English language—Rhythm. I. Strong, William. II. Title.
    LB1576.S852   1999
    372.6—dc21   98-51502
                                                           CIP

Printed in the United States of America

Illustrations drawn under contract by Nora Voutas

Cover design by Kris Gausman

THINKING PUBLICATIONS®
A Division of McKinley Companies, Inc.

424 Galloway Street • Eau Claire, WI 54703
715-832-2488 • FAX 715-832-9082
Email: custserv@ThinkingPublications.com

COMMUNICATION SOLUTIONS THAT CHANGE LIVES®

For Tori and Will Strong, beginners on the long, happy path of language learning, as they enjoy the rhymes and stories told by their mom and dad

ABOUT THE AUTHORS

Carol J. Strong, a professor in the Department of Communicative Disorders and Deaf Education at Utah State University, teaches courses in language and emergent literacy development, language assessment and intervention, language disorders of school-aged students, and educational and psychological research. In 1989, she received an American Speech-Language-Hearing Association (ASHA) Foundation research award for new investigators; in 1991, her work was recognized by the American Association of University Women in Utah with an Emerging Scholar Award; in 1995, she received the Editor's Award from ASHA for the article of highest merit published in *Language, Speech, and Hearing Services in Schools*, which served as the foundation for her 1996 book, *The Magic of Stories*, coauthored with Kelly Hoggan North; and in 1998, she received the Professor of the Year Award from Utah State University. Ten years of school-based clinical research following her doctoral dissertation study led to the publication of the *Strong Narrative Assessment Procedure (SNAP)* in 1998. Also, she has presented numerous workshops, seminars, and technical papers at state, national, and international conferences focused on enhancing language and literacy in children with language impairments.

William Strong directs the Utah Writing Project at Utah State University, where he is head of the Department of Secondary Education and teaches courses in writing, content area reading, and English education. In addition to this book, his resource materials include *Sentence Combining: A Composing Book* (1973, 1983, 1994), *Sentence Combining and Paragraph Building* (1981), *Practicing Sentence Options* (1984), *Crafting Cumulative Sentences* (1984), *Mastering Basic Vocabulary* (1984), *Writing Incisively: Do-It-Yourself Prose Surgery* (1991), and *Writer's Toolbox* (1996). His monograph, *Creative Approaches to Sentence Combining* (1986), provides an introduction to the theory, research, and practice associated with the approach. Also, he is the consulting author in composition for *Writer's Choice* (1993, 1996), a Glencoe/McGraw-Hill textbook series for grades 9–12. In 1988, he received an award for teaching excellence at Utah State University; in 1990, he was honored by the Utah Council of Teachers of English for his service to the state; and in 1998, he received the Distinguished Service Award from the Utah Association of Teacher Educators. In addition to working with teachers of writing at all levels, he enjoys downhill skiing, gardening, and motorcycle touring with Carol Strong.

CONTENTS

PREFACE

When our granddaughter Tori was 25 months old, her parents moved from Las Vegas to Seattle in an epic summer journey indelibly etched in Strong family history. Tori sat strapped in her car seat, surrounded by her favorite books and stuffed animals. In the rear of the Jeep Cherokee, badly overloaded like the truck in *The Grapes of Wrath*, rode three stir-crazy cats.

To help with this 1,000 mile move, Grandma Strong bounced along in the Jeep's stiff back seat reading (and, alas, rereading) Tori's favorite "pop-up" book, *Love Bugs*, (1995) by D.A. Carter. One pop-up page always prompted a memorized joyful chant from Tori: "About one thing I have no doubt!" Grandma's task was to say the anticipated response line: "The love bug will bite you if you don't watch out!"

To vary the exchange—and maintain sanity—Grandma soon began substituting the names of stuffed animals, relatives, and caged cats for the expected "love bug" phrase—as in "Elmo will bite you if you don't watch out!" For countless repetitions over at least 100 miles, Grandma and Tori continued this game, Tori chanting her line and Grandma chanting hers. It was somewhere out on the wild, windswept outback of western Nevada that Grandma tried to substitute "get you" in the chanted response line. "No!" Tori corrected. "Big Bird will *bite* me!"

We open with this story because of the questions it raises. Why, we ask, did a child of only 25 months so love this "drill-and-practice" exchange? What aspects of language did she rehearse and internalize, mile after mile? As teachers, how might we invite similar—though more developmentally sophisticated—practice in classrooms and clinics?

In our view, the strong rhythm and rhyme of this chant engaged Tori. Although it was highly predictable, the chant also had surprises as words from Tori's lexicon were playfully introduced. The back-and-forth social exchange was one that Tori enjoyed and to a large extent controlled. Had she been a little older, she would surely have switched roles with Grandma to control the exchange even further.

Whatever the cause for her interest and enjoyment, Tori was clearly gaining practice and tacit knowledge of intertwined language and emergent literacy skills—among them, rhyming, word segmentation and substitution, complex syntax, future tense auxiliary forms, and negation. Her "correction" of Grandma's modification showed that she fully understood the pragmatics of the exchange, as she substituted "bite me" for the expected phrase "bite you."

The three introductory chapters of this resource book explain in detail the rationale for a new form of chanting activity, one created by children as they combine given sentences. Although sentence-combining chants are more complex than the back-seat exchange of Tori and Grandma Strong, they have much the same spirit of playful and rhythmic predictability. It is our contention that such rhyming chants provide the occasion for facilitating phonological awareness as well as the use of advanced syntactic structures.

We appreciate the cooperation of April Newton and Audra Hunsaker at Lincoln Elementary School in Hyrum, Utah, in the trials of lessons from *Strong Rhythms and Rhymes*. Thanks also to the students who participated so enthusiastically. We appreciate the contributions of Willis Pitkin in serving as our linguistic consultant.

We are grateful for the support of Nancy McKinley, editor in chief at Thinking Publications; Linda Schreiber, senior editor; Angie Orth and Sarah Tobalsky, editors; and their able production staff. Kudos also for the contributions of our external reviewer, Sue Schultz.

Best wishes as you use the materials in this book. We welcome your comments about chanting activities, especially those that might assist other teachers or clinicians with practical day-to-day matters. Please correspond with us at the following address:

Carol J. Strong, Ed.D.
Department of Communicative Disorders and Deaf Education
Utah State University
Logan, UT 84322-1000
Email: carols@coe.usu.edu

Part I
Introduction

Chapter 1
The Magic of Chanting

Just for fun, think about the following list of titles:

- "Happy Birthday"
- "Mary Had a Little Lamb"
- "Two-Four-Six-Eight"

In reading these titles, do you hear words and rhythms from years gone by? How about "Little Jack Horner"? Or "Old MacDonald"? Do these titles also evoke memorized language structures?

We ask such questions because we believe that rhythm and rhyme facilitate the rehearsal and mastery of a variety of language features essential to spoken and written communication. As a teacher of young children, you have no doubt seen many examples of such rehearsal in natural contexts, such as

- repeating and rhyming words at bedtime;
- chanting jump rope or hopscotch rhymes;
- singing jingles from television commercials;
- repeating and dancing to rap music lyrics;
- chanting a slogan or cheer for a school club or team; and
- composing limericks or rhymes just for fun.

Sentence-combining chant exercises blend rhythm and rhyme with the presentation of targeted syntactic structures so that children acquire the structures in a more natural context.

Children with intact neurological systems seem naturally motivated to engage in rhythm and rhyme activities with little prompting. Infants, for example, love to participate in interactive chants like "Pat-a-Cake" or "The Itsy-Bitsy Spider"—or to be bounced on an adult knee as "Humpty Dumpty" is chanted. There is great pleasure for children in linking a strong, rhythmic beat to familiar words (McCracken and McCracken, 1986).

Another attraction of chanting is its social quality—the individual voice mingled with the voices of others. Internalizing the content and structure of a new language form (learning the "Pledge of Allegiance," for example) involves subordinating one's voice to the voice of the group. The group activity provides support, or scaffolding, for the language-learning individual. Such support is critical for students who are learning English as a second language or who are delayed in language-skill development (Buchoff, 1994).

When chanting is linked with reading and writing, it provides a supportive bridge for the development of early literacy skills. A newly introduced chant can be read, however haltingly, by beginning readers. The rehearsal of the chant reinforces and supports reading fluency, especially as the chant becomes memorized. By the same token, a memorized chant can be transcribed by students during a writing activity. This writing, in turn, can serve as the springboard for drawing, talking, role-playing, and further creative work, such as story or poetry writing (Strong and Strong, 1994).

Overview

Strong Rhythms and Rhymes: Language and Literacy Development Through Sentence Combining provides 100 sentence-combining chant exercises to assist students with the development of phonological awareness and syntax skills. Helping students develop phonological awareness is essential to the oral language foundation on which subsequent literacy is built. Similarly, helping students comprehend and use more complex syntax makes them better communicators and prepares them for reading and writing instruction. The nature and importance of phonological awareness is explained more fully in Chapter 2, and a developmental ladder of syntax is presented in Chapter 3.

Sentence combining is a versatile tool for creative teaching, not merely a skill-and-drill activity. As students combine sentences to create snap-happy rhythms and clap-happy rhymes, they learn new language structures playfully and naturally, without grammatical terms. Sentence-combining chants should have much the same spirit as a jump-rope rhyme or rap on the playground.

Students naturally rehearse language when it feels good and when it is reinforced by the social context (in this case, peers, teachers, and family members). Therefore, the chants in this resource have been written to appeal to young language learners. Each chant is accompanied by a visual illustration and includes a "strong" element of humor. Such content appeals are supported by research (Norton, 1991) as well as by common sense and our own work with students in classroom and clinical settings. Indeed, the more bizarre the exercise, the more it seems to lodge in the consciousness of students, amusing and educating them.

4

Strong Rhythms and Rhymes is divided into two major sections and also includes appendixes, references, and indexes for educator use. Part I is comprised of Chapter 1, which provides an overview of the resource, a rationale for using chanting and sentence combining, and a four-step teaching approach for using the provided exercises; Chapter 2, which contains information on phonological awareness; and Chapter 3, which discusses syntax development.

Part II provides 100 alphabetically organized chant exercises. Each exercise in Part II is numbered and includes two pages: one for educator use and one for students. The educator page provides a chant model; syntax goals; the rhyme family(ies); teaching ideas (introductory sharing, vocabulary targets, and an extension activity); and space to document comments, observations, and additional teaching ideas pertaining to the exercise. The student page includes a visual representation of the chant and the four kernel-sentence pairs with corresponding sentence-closure clues. The illustrated student page can be duplicated and either displayed or distributed to students for use during the lesson.

Following Part II are the appendixes and indexes. The appendixes include example goals and objectives, which could be used to develop individualized educational programs (IEPs). The appendixes also contain the materials to use when introducing chanting and sentence combining to students, as well as a recording form for monitoring development of syntactic structures. The indexes include *Title Index, Developmental Level Index, Rhyme Family Index,* and *Syntactic Structure Index.* Each of these indexes is described more fully in Chapter 1. All of the features of this resource have been designed for ease of use by busy educators. The heart of this resource is the abundant practice material for reinforcing phonological awareness and for developing more advanced syntactic structures.

Target Audience

Strong Rhythms and Rhymes contains 100 sentence-combining chant exercises that are designed for students in first through sixth grade, as well as for students needing language development in clinical or special education settings. Preschool and kindergarten students can also enjoy and profit from oral chanting activities. English as a second language teachers will find these exercises a useful skill-building activity for speakers struggling with English vocabulary and syntax. Exercises may be used with large or small groups of students or with individual learners in one-on-one settings.

Chanting as a Scaffolding Activity

Chanting is a means to an end—improved phonological awareness, syntactic fluency, and joyful expression—not an end in itself. Chanting provides a scaffold, or support, for skill development.

This teaching premise derives from ideas articulated by Lev Vygotsky (1978), the great Russian psychologist and student of language development.

The concept of a "zone of proximal development" (ZPD) may be Vygotsky's single greatest contribution to language research and teaching. Basically, Vygotsky (1962) argued that "the only good kind of instruction is that which marches ahead of development and leads it" (p. 104). He defined the ZPD as the difference between two levels of linguistic or cognitive performance—that which the student can do independently and that which he or she can do with the help of an adult or more capable peers. Vygotsky's main assertion was that whatever students can do today with assistance, they will eventually be able to do on their own. Students use the social support to internalize new concepts and skills.

Chants are clearly a playful, social activity. In clinics or classrooms, students solve problems in sentence combining with the help of an adult or more capable peers. This social activity will heighten phonological awareness and introduce syntactic structures not yet within the student's spoken or written repertoire. Through chanting, students orally rehearse, as in a song or jump-rope rhyme, new concepts and structures. What the student has memorized and committed to "inner speech" can then be transcribed; this further reinforces the use of more advanced structures. Transcribed language, in turn, can serve as the foundation for talking, drawing, dramatic activity, or further writing.

Gallimore and Tharp (1990), in their discussion of Vygotsky, defined teaching as "assisted performance." When meaningful sentence-combining work is presented by teachers in an appealing way, it becomes an ideal activity setting for collaborative language learning. Sentence-combining practice helps students internalize a variety of sentence patterns associated with written discourse (e.g., Hunt, 1977; Strong, 1986). With access to more mature syntax and an increased ability to hold language in short-term memory during transcription, students profit from reading and writing instruction.

Any approach to language instruction and intervention has limitations. Language acquisition is a highly complex act of personal construction. Nevertheless, educators can do much to assist students in linguistically helpful ways. *Strong Rhythms and Rhymes* makes the exposure to, and rehearsal of, linguistic structures and phonological elements more natural and automatic. Students engage in learning through multiple modalities, increasing the likelihood that skills will be acquired and maintained. Finally, students have fun while participating in the chant exercises, which greatly aids in their active learning.

It is important to remember the larger context for skill development. Students should participate in daily read-aloud activities in which adults introduce them to the joys of age-appropriate literature as well as advanced syntax and vocabulary. Also, students should frequently select stories and texts to share with friends and compose their own stories and poems.

Krashen (1984) described such activities as "comprehensible input"—that is, large amounts of meaningful oral interchange coupled with "large amounts of self-motivated reading for interest and/or pleasure" (p. 20). Collaborative problem-solving activities in which students rehearse syntactic structures may serve as another source of "comprehensible input," especially for students needing additional support for language learning.

How Sentence Combining Works

Each student page of a chant exercise consists of four pairs of kernel sentences, plus closure clues for sentence combining. (Refer to Figure 1 on page 8 for an example student page.) Closure clues are the blank lines and cue words that accompany each sentence pair. The goal of the activity is for students to read or listen to the kernel sentences and then combine each sentence pair into a single, more complex sentence. Visual, auditory, and social scaffolds assist students with the combining task.

Because all exercises follow the same pattern, students come to use rhythm and rhyme as support for combining sentences. With a little instruction and practice, students tend to naturally "fill in the blanks" from the context of given information (the kernel sentences), and from the activity of chanting, either in unison or individually. The combined sentence chant for the example provided in Figure 1 is as follows:

> *I love chanting line by line.*
> *When I chant, I feel so fine.*
> *I take chants and make them mine.*
> *Oh, I love chanting line by line!*

Although this chant may seem simple, consider the rhythmic drilling of phonological awareness for young learners in the following phrases: (1) *line by line*, (2) *feel so fine*, (3) *make them mine*, (4) *line by line*. Notice first how the rhyming words are reinforced by alliteration—the repetition of initial consonant sounds in each line. Now focus on *take* and *make* as well as *so* and *oh*, the additional internal rhymes in lines 2, 3, and 4. Finally, consider the noun and verb forms of the word *chant*, each signaled by context and inflectional endings in lines 1, 2, 3, and 4. Clearly, much is happening in four short lines. The chant is fun and interesting because its rhythmic and rhyming features engage phonological skills. Chapter 2 further discusses the role of phonological awareness in these activities and in literacy development.

Chant 9: Chanting

I love chanting.

I chant line by line.   line _____.

I chant.   When _____,

I feel so fine.   _____.

I take chants.   _____

I make them mine.   and _____.

I love chanting.   Oh, _____

I chant line by line.   _____!

© 1999 Thinking Publications. Duplication permitted for educational use only.   59

Figure 1 _Example Student Page_

In addition to developing phonological awareness, sentence combining can help students learn many syntax structures in a relaxed and playful way, particularly as exercises are solved, then repeated and memorized. For example, the chant exercise shown in Figure 1 reinforces three language transformations: adverb phrase embedding (lines 1 and 4), adverb clause subordination (line 2), and coordination of verb phrases (line 3). The aim of introducing and reinforcing target structures is to help students move up the developmental ladder of syntax. (The developmental ladder of syntax is discussed more fully in Chapter 3.) Once target structures have been introduced and practiced in sentence-combining exercises, they can be reinforced in other classroom or clinical activities, such as reading, writing, and storytelling. Possible extension activities are described later in this chapter (see pages 19–20).

How to Use This Resource

Before using _Strong Rhythms and Rhymes_ with students, review Chapter 2, which discusses the role and importance of phonological awareness, and Chapter 3, which describes a developmental ladder of syntax. Then, introduce the idea of chanting to students and prepare them for sentence-combining exercises. (Activities for introducing the concept of chanting and preparing students for chant exercises are provided next.)

Determine relevant rhyme families based on individual needs of students and/or general classroom curriculum, activities, and themes. The _Rhyme Family Index_ indicates which rhyme family(ies) is targeted by each exercise. Locate the desired rhyme family in the index and select from the corresponding exercise(s) within Part II.

Determine relevant syntactic structures for students. Syntax needs can be determined in several ways, including formal language testing, informal language sample analysis, and review of students' portfolios or files. *Example Goals and Objectives* (Appendix A) can be useful in writing syntax needs in an objective format. The *Syntactic Structure Index* shows the syntactic structure targets in each exercise, and whether each structure appears in a phrase or clause. Locate the desired syntactic structure(s) in the index, and select from the corresponding exercise(s) within Part II. Start with chants rated as *easy* (E), gradually moving on to chants rated *moderate* (M) and *difficult* (D) as students seem ready.

After selecting appropriate chant exercises based on rhyme families and syntactic structures, preview the chants that introduce and emphasize these chosen targets. Choose a chant for use and conduct the accompanying exercise. Lessons should be conducted using the four-step teaching paradigm described on pages 11–20.

Preparing Students for Chant Exercises

Sentence combining may be a new activity for students. If this is the case, it is important to prepare them, so that they feel success from the outset. Perhaps the best way to introduce sentence combining is through several demonstrations of increasing difficulty.

1. Duplicate "A Famous Story #1" and "Jack and Jill," from Appendix B, onto an overhead transparency, or write the stories on a chalkboard or flip chart. Read "A Famous Story #1" aloud to students as a set of declarative sentences.

   A Famous Story #1

   Jack went up the hill.
   Jill went up the hill.
   They went to fetch a pail.
   Water was in the pail.
   Jack fell down.
   He broke his crown.
   Jill came tumbling after him.

2. After reading "A Famous Story #1" to the class, ask students how many of them have heard this story before. Ask if they have heard another version of the same story. Ask if anyone could say aloud the similar story they have heard.

3. In response to these questions, one or more students will probably volunteer the name of the Mother Goose rhyme "Jack and Jill." If no one volunteers the expected response, provide it for the class orally. Then, present "A Famous Story #1" side-by-side with the combined version titled "Jack and Jill."

Jack and Jill

Jack and Jill went up the hill
To fetch a pail of water.
Jack fell down and broke his crown,
And Jill came tumbling after.

Ask students about the differences they notice between the two versions. Help them see that although the stories contain the same information, the second one is shorter and more interesting than the first one. Ask students why this might be so. Help students see that the second version has combined sentences, whereas the first one has short, choppy sentences. Explain that putting sentences together is not only fun but also worth doing, because by combining sentences in new ways, people improve their speaking, reading, and writing.

4. Keeping the version of "Jack and Jill" displayed so all can see, help the students chant the rhyme. Model and encourage clapping, snapping, or tapping while chanting.

5. Write the word *chanting* where all students can see it and discuss the term. Discuss other forms of chants, including jump-rope rhymes, raps, songs, and cheers for school teams.

6. Next, duplicate and display "A Famous Story #2," from Appendix B, on an overhead transparency, or write it on a chalkboard or flip chart. This story is set up as a sentence-combining chant, complete with closure clues. Help students combine the sentences using the closure clues. As students read the kernel sentences and fill in the closure clues using a familiar story, they develop a better understanding of the structure and expectations of other chants. Model and encourage clapping, snapping, or tapping while chanting the newly combined sentences for "The Itsy-Bitsy Spider."

7. At this point, try introducing an easy exercise like *Chant 9: Chanting* (pages 58–59) as a choral activity. Duplicate the student page as an overhead transparency or as a handout. Before distributing or displaying the student page, have students repeat each of the four target (i.e., combined) sentences, so that they feel the rhythm and structure of the exercise. Display the student page and/or distribute the handout. Point out that, just like in "A Famous Story #2," there are eight short sentences as well as some hints for combining them. Read the eight sentences aloud, and explain that the goal of the activity is to combine sentences so that they make a rhyming chant. See if students can recall the four target sentences repeated earlier to fill in the sentence frames. Finally, perform the newly made chant with the students.

8. After students have been exposed to the introductory chants, explain that they will be participating in many new activities for sentence combining. Enlist the cooperation of students in solving the "puzzles" in sentence combining. Explain to students that some parts of the exercises might seem tough at times, but that the chants will always be fun and interesting once they are "solved." Also explain that it is all right to make mistakes while learning. Encouraging students to take risks with sentence combining helps them relax. Language is most effectively learned when students feel safe. A safe environment helps young children pay attention to the language tasks at hand.

A Four-Step Teaching Approach

Chant exercises should be taught after students have been introduced to the concepts of chanting and sentence combining. The chants in *Strong Rhythms and Rhymes* should be distributed over many days, weeks, or months rather than taught all at once for long periods of time. Try to keep the chanting a fresh, lively activity that students enjoy and look forward to. Figure 2 summarizes the four-step teaching approach for conducting these sentence-combining exercises.

Four-Step Teaching Paradigm for Chant Exercises

1. Preview and plan instruction.

2. Demonstrate the sentence-combining task.

3. Involve students in varied chanting.

4. Extend the chant exercise.

Figure 2 *Four-Step Teaching Approach*

Preview and Plan Instruction

As an example of previewing and planning instruction, refer to the educator and student pages for *Chant 21: Fred the Frog*, presented as Figure 3 on page 12. The educator page is intended as a reference for planning a chant exercise. Notice the different elements of this page.

The "Chant Model" section of the educator page provides the end goal—the target sentences—for the sentence-combining exercise. This is the only place where the completed, four-line chant model occurs. Refer to the chant model prior to the lesson to view the intended combined sentences.

ₛₜᵣₒₙg**Rhythms**=**Rhymes** ──────────────

Chant 21: Fred the Frog   **Level = D**

Chant Model   **Syntax Goals**

Chant Model		Syntax Goals	
Fred is a frog that jumps on the bed.	Line 1	Subordination (relative—*that*)	Clause
With a quick kick, he lands on my head.	Line 2	Preposition embedding *(with)*	Phrase
His trick is slick, so he can get fed.	Line 3	Subordination (adverbial—*so [that]*)	Clause
Oh, Fred is a frog that jumps on the bed!	Line 4	Subordination (relative—*that*)	Clause

Rhyme Families

[-ed] *bed, fed, Fred, head*
[-ick] *kick, quick, slick, trick*
[-is] *his, is*
[-ow] *oh, so*

Teaching Ideas

Introductory Sharing: pets; frogs as pets; pets that do tricks for food
Vocabulary Targets: *quick kick, trick, "slick," fed*
Extension Activity: Using a stuffed toy frog, demonstrate hopping, jumping, and landing.

Comments, Observations, and Additional Teaching Ideas

3/25/99—Jessie told about frogs he had seen during a family camping trip. Remember to bridge the frog discussion to the camping unit in May.

82

Illustrated Student Page (page 83):

Chant 21: Fred the Frog

Fred is a frog.   _____
He jumps on the bed.   that _____.

He makes a quick kick.   With _____,
He lands on my head.   he _____.

His trick is slick.   _____,
He can get fed.   so _____.

Fred is a frog.   Oh, _____
He jumps on the bed.   _____!

83

Figure 3 *Educator Page and Illustrated Student Page for* Chant 21: Fred the Frog

Refer to the "Syntax Goals" section prior to the lesson to recognize the desired syntactic targets for the chant exercise. For syntax goals, notice that *Fred the Frog* targets three transformations: relative clause subordination *(that)*, prepositional phrase embedding *(with)*, and adverbial clause subordination *(so,* a reduction of *so that)*. Notice that the relative clause is cued in the first sentence but uncued in the fourth sentence. Students supply the second *that* connector from memory by repeating the first sentence. Technical grammatical terms are not used to prompt students in their use of skills. What counts is the students' use of language, not their mastery of grammatical terms.

For ease of use in classrooms and clinics, only one syntax goal is stated for each pair of kernel sentences, even when another transformation occurs during the sentence combining. In creating compound subjects, for example, children must link nouns with *and,* but must also change verb forms for purposes of agreement. This total process is referred to as "coordination."

Refer to the "Rhyme Families" section when planning phonological awareness extension questions. Notice the rhyme families in the *Fred the Frog* chant (e.g., –ed—*bed/fed/Fred/head;* –ick—*kick/quick/slick/trick).* Encourage students to brainstorm other words in the same rhyme families by substituting consonants and consonant blends in appropriate slots (e.g., ___*ed* and ___*ick).*

In addition to full rhymes, many near rhymes are woven into the chants to enrich the activities. For example, in *Chant 11: Cool Cat,* you will find four full rhymes in the [-at] family: *at, cat, hat,* and *Matt.* Also included is a near rhyme: *ratty.* Technically, this is an assonantal rhyme or slant rhyme. When near rhymes occur, explain to the students how part of one word (e.g., *rat-* in *ratty)* rhymes with the other words (e.g., *at, cat).*

Scan the "Teaching Ideas" section before teaching each exercise to stimulate your thinking about how the chant might be effectively introduced and taught. There are three teaching idea elements for each chant exercise.

1. The Introductory Sharing element describes topics that could be discussed to initiate the exercise. In the Introductory Sharing element for *Fred the Frog,* there are three recommended ideas: talking about pets, discussing frogs as pets, and talking about pets that do tricks for food. When preparing an introduction for this exercise, you might consider asking the students how many of them have pets. Do they know any students who have unusual pets? What kinds of tricks do pets perform for food? How would they like a frog as a pet? Planning such questions will help you activate students' background knowledge for the exercise.

2. The Vocabulary Targets element identifies key terms used within the exercise. Consider the vocabulary targets when preparing materials for each exercise. When possible, bring in pictures or actual objects to depict words that may be new or may require clarification. Plan to discuss multiple meaning words, homonyms, figurative expressions, synonyms, antonyms, etc. that arise within the lesson. Figurative expressions are indicated with quotation marks. Plan to use an overhead projector, a chalkboard, or a flip chart to present key words and pictures in a list, semantic web, or other type of vocabulary graphic. Consider having the students role-play action words. For the chant *Fred the Frog,* plan to clarify and discuss vocabulary such as *quick kick,* "*slick,*" and *fed.*

3. The third teaching element included is an Extension Activity. Planning for an extension activity might involve bridging the exercise to another upcoming classroom event or activity. An extension activity might arise from particular interests expressed by students themselves. Or the activity might involve reading related children's literature to students.

An extension activity for the chant *Fred the Frog* is to bring in a stuffed toy frog puppet for students to use at another time during the day (e.g., during free time or music time). Students could be encouraged to demonstrate hopping, jumping, and landing. Activities often grow naturally out of a sharing discussion or through vocabulary work. For example, one or more students may want to draw a picture of a frog or imitate its croak.

Also, plan for extension questions that emphasize phonological awareness. For example, ask the students, "What sound is at the end of the word *frog?*" Follow up with a direction to "think of words that rhyme with *frog.*" List these words on an overhead projector, chalkboard, or flip chart. Extension activities that relate to and develop phonological awareness skills may include the following:

- rhyming new words to key/target words
- segmenting words within sentences (counting words)
- segmenting words into syllables (counting syllables)
- segmenting sounds within words (counting sounds)
- identifying sounds (phonemes) and their corresponding letters (graphemes)

The section "Comments, Observations, and Additional Teaching Ideas" is provided for taking notes about other sharing, vocabulary, or extension activities that were especially useful during the chant exercise. Also, notes pertaining to the content of the discussions prior to, during, and following the chant exercise could be recorded. In the example of *Fred the Frog* presented in Figure 3 on page 12, observations regarding how one student volunteered ideas about tricky pets or how another student talked about frogs he had seen on a family camping trip were worthwhile to record for future planning. Comments and notes can provide "hooks" for future exercises, helping students become involved. By connecting a new lesson with one from the past, meaningful connections for students are made. Notes will also save time when planning for future chant exercises. Write in this section each time a chant exercise is conducted.

Prior to teaching a chant exercise, prepare either an overhead transparency and/or student handouts from the illustrated student page provided for the selected chant. An advantage of using a transparency accompanied by handouts is that students can imitate on their copies the writing you do on the overhead transparency. Also, students can collect handouts in folders and take them home to read aloud to parents and siblings. In this way, each student develops a personal anthology of chants.

Lastly, before conducting the first chant exercise with students, prepare one photocopy of the *Recording Form for Syntactic Structures* (see Appendix C) for each student. The procedures for using this form as a monitoring device are discussed on pages 20–21.

Demonstrate the Sentence-Combining Task

Use the material in the "Teaching Ideas" section to introduce the chant to the class. It may take five minutes or more to build background knowledge for the exercise. This time is well spent because it teaches essential skills and builds interest and motivation.

Tell students that people can make longer sentences from short, choppy sentences when they speak or write. Explain that using the longer sentences can make it easier to communicate when speaking and writing.

Show students the kernel sentences to be combined by placing the illustrated student page on an overhead projector or by writing the sentences and closure clues on a chalkboard or flip chart. Encourage students first to read the kernel sentences in their uncombined form, on the left side of the student page. Read all eight sentences aloud. Invite student volunteers to read individual sentences, or have the class read all eight sentences in unison. Encourage students to follow along on their handouts, if provided. In the example of *Fred the Frog*, the following kernel sentences would be read:

Fred is a frog.
He jumps on the bed.
He makes a quick kick.
He lands on my head.
His trick is slick.
He can get fed.
Fred is a frog.
He jumps on the bed.

It is important to demonstrate the sentence-combining task to give students a clear sense of what is expected. A high level of demonstration is essential for students who have language-learning disabilities, limited English proficiency, or other language problems.

Ask students to keep time by clapping, snapping, or tapping their fingers on their desktops. When everyone is rhythmically together, combine the first two sentences orally for the students, following the established four-beat rhythm. Then, while students continue their clapping, snapping, or tapping, write the combined sentence on the overhead transparency, chalkboard, or flip chart. Finally, encourage students to chant the new, complex sentence together with you for two or three repetitions. Continue this procedure for the remaining sentence pairs. (For subsequent chant exercises, as the students become familiar with the procedure, ask volunteers to guess the new combined sentence form for each kernel-sentence pair.) When all four pairs of sentences are combined, perform the chant several times as a group. (See pages 17–19 for ways to vary the chant activity.)

When students understand the structure of the sentence-combining task, you will probably prefer a less directive approach, one that engages students in figuring out how sentences are combined. For example, try inviting volunteers to use the "cue words" to put the sentences together on their own (without chanting). Students can work in pairs to figure out the transformations and then volunteer these responses to the group. Such problem solving helps students develop confidence, skill, and cooperative-learning strategies.

Encourage students with positive responses, such as, "Good job! Let me help you with that one," even when they produce only slightly flawed sentences. It is important to encourage all responses, so that students will be attentive and engaged in future lessons. The goal at this stage is involvement, not perfection. Although the rhythm and rhyme of the chants produce a scripted outcome, slight variations are acceptable. For example, in line 3 of *Fred the Frog*, some students might say, "His trick is slick, so *that* he can get fed."

Clapping, snapping, tapping feet, and bobbing shoulders make chanting fun. Over time, develop your own cues for helping students begin the chant together. When starting out, the following three-step cue might be useful:

"Okay, class, let's all begin the chant after we click our fingers and count to four. Ready? Count with me, please." (Using an exaggerated downbeat cue, count and snap simultaneously to model what you expect.) *"1–2–3–4."* (Each snap should emphasize the boldfaced words below as you rhythmically chant *Fred the Frog*.)

Fred is a **frog** that **jumps** on the **bed**.
With a quick **kick**, he **lands** on my **head**.
His **trick** is **slick**, so **he** can get **fed**.
Oh, **Fred** is a **frog** that **jumps** on the **bed**!

A visual downbeat cue on the boldfaced words assists students in keeping the rhythm going. If students have difficulty with chanting in unison, try leaving the written chant script visible for the class, so that it can be read rhythmically. If the exercise still seems too difficult, select an easier chant for the next exercise. With just a little practice, most students quickly catch on to chanting activities. Once the routine is established, no further "how-to" instruction should be necessary.

Repeat the process described above with different chant exercises over a period of days until students are comfortable with chanting. The chants can begin at a slow or moderate tempo, then speed up as soon as they are learned. Gradually fade your voice so that the students' voices dominate.

After students are comfortable with chanting, point out how the given connectors assist with sentence combining and how extra words are sometimes deleted to make the combined sentences.

This teaching involves comparing the kernel sentences with the combined sentences. In some chants (e.g., *Chant 13: Cutoff Jeans*), the word *something* functions as a "slot" or "placeholder" for noun clause transformations. For example:

Let us tell you something.	*Let us tell you* _____
This means something.	what *this means* _____ .

When *something* serves such a function, it must be deleted to combine the sentences. Some students may be perplexed by this deletion, wondering about the word. Explain to students that they can put new ideas in place of the word *something*. Other deletion transformations may require similar explanation. Also, use of brackets, [ ], will be noticed in the "Syntax Goals" section of the educator page. For example, *[that]*, *so [that]*, or *[in order] to* appear at times. The bracketed material refers to words that are understood but not spoken. By bracketing words in this way, the underlying transformations are apparent. To keep the chant rhythmic, the words in brackets are not voiced.

Following the exercise, refer back to the *Recording Form for Syntactic Structures* duplicated earlier. Indicate each student's level of performance for each targeted syntactic structure during the sentence combining and chanting. (See pages 20–21 for a detailed description.)

Involve Students in Varied Chanting

After students have mastered the routine for unison chanting, you can vary the chanting and involve students in different ways. With an *echo approach*, for example, students simply repeat a leader's chant. The leader can be the educator or another student. The back-and-forth practice of two sets of voices creates an effect different from a traditional unison chant. The following example demonstrates the echo format using the *Fred the Frog* chant.

LEADER: **Fred** is a **frog** that **jumps** on the **bed.**
STUDENTS: **Fred** is a **frog** that **jumps** on the **bed.**
LEADER: **With** a quick **kick,** he **lands** on my **head.**
STUDENTS: **With** a quick **kick,** he **lands** on my **head.**
LEADER: His **trick** is **slick,** so **he** can get **fed.**
STUDENTS: His **trick** is **slick,** so **he** can get **fed.**
LEADER: Oh, **Fred** is a **frog** that **jumps** on the **bed!**
STUDENTS: Oh, **Fred** is a **frog** that **jumps** on the **bed!**

Using this format, experiment with whispers—the leader's whisper echoed by students' whispers, the leader's whisper followed by students' normal volume, or the leader's normal volume followed by students' whispers. Consider echoing a whisper with an increasingly louder volume.

A *two-voice approach* has the students completing the second half of each sentence. This format can be reversed so that the students lead and you follow. Also, students can do this chant format in pairs, on their own. The following example demonstrates the two-voice format using the *Fred the Frog* chant.

LEADER: **Fred** is a **frog**

STUDENTS: that **jumps** on the **bed.**

LEADER: **With** a quick **kick,**

STUDENTS: he **lands** on my **head.**

LEADER: His **trick** is **slick,**

STUDENTS: so **he** can get **fed.**

LEADER: Oh, **Fred** is a **frog**

STUDENTS: that **jumps** on the **bed!**

Another way to vary the two-voice approach is to chant alternate lines. Again, this approach also works well for students in pairs. The following example demonstrates the varied two-voice format with the *Fred the Frog* chant.

LEADER: **Fred** is a **frog** that **jumps** on the **bed.**

STUDENTS: **With** a quick **kick,** he **lands** on my **head.**

LEADER: His **trick** is **slick,** so **he** can get **fed.**

STUDENTS: Oh, **Fred** is a **frog** that **jumps** on the **bed!**

A more complex two-voice variation is a *chaining voices approach*. This is done by pointing to each other or by passing around an object, such as a toy frog. Organize students into small circled groups and have them begin clapping, snapping, or gently tapping their desktops. Initiate the activity by saying a chant line and "passing" to a student who adds a line and passes to someone else. Passing refers to pointing to, looking at, or handing an object to the person who is to chant next. The group keeps time as each speaker contributes to the chant or to a sequence of memorized chants. The chaining serves to reinforce target transformations.

After a given exercise has been memorized by students, consider using a fifth, more dif-ficult, approach called *rounds*. "Row, Row, Row Your Boat" is commonly done as a round. Divide students into four groups and practice "Row, Row, Row Your Boat" in rounds until students are comfortable with the activity. The following is the chant pattern to use.

Row, row, row your boat. Gently down the stream;
Merrily, merrily, merrily, merrily. Life is but a dream!
(Repeat two times.)

GROUP 1: Row, row, row your boat…

GROUP 2: Row, row, row your boat…

GROUP 3: Row, row, row your boat…

GROUP 4: Row, row, row your boat…

After the students are comfortable using the rounds format with "Row, Row, Row Your Boat," direct them to practice a different chant using the same approach. The following is the format for beginning round chanting for *Fred the Frog*.

GROUP 1: Fred is a frog that jumps on the bed.…

GROUP 2: Fred is a frog that jumps on the bed.…

GROUP 3: Fred is a frog that jumps on the bed.…

GROUP 4: Fred is a frog that jumps on the bed.…

Students often enjoy a progression in which they move from a whisper in the first round, to a loud voice the final time through the chant, or vice versa.

Finally, vary chant exercises by having students lead the chants. When working with a small group of students, assign each a different chant to lead. Then perform the chants in sequence, with each student taking responsibility for the leadership of one chant (e.g., standing in front of the group, snapping his or her fingers, giving the downbeat cue). In this way, the chants blend together over a period of several minutes. Remember, too, that a leadership activity can often help address behavior difficulties with some students.

Extend the Chant Exercise

Once students have completed a few repetitions of a chant, they will likely be able to recite it from memory, without glancing at a written copy. Because they hear language in their heads, students should be able to transcribe the chant. Encourage students to whisper the chant to themselves as they transcribe it on a blank sheet of paper. Then ask them to check their capitalization, spelling, and punctuation against a completed illustrated student page and to make changes as necessary. As a variation, students could proof each other's transcriptions prior to checking against the original copy of the chant.

Students can use chants as springboards for sentence elaboration and creative writing. The sentences that have been chanted and transcribed serve as syntactic and imaginative scaffolding for writing and subsequent reading. Invite students to draw pictures to go with their four-sentence story. Then ask students to share their illustrations and explain their ideas. The pictures force students to visualize and to make explicit what they imagine. Encourage extensions of the stories that students imagine. For example, to facilitate sentence expansion, initiate an exchange such as the following:

EDUCATOR: How could you describe what you see in your drawing?

STUDENT: Fred is a big green frog that jumps on the bunk bed.

EDUCATOR: That's great! Write that down.

To prompt further thinking or imagination, initiate an exchange such as:

EDUCATOR: What kind of food do you suppose Fred eats?

STUDENT: I don't know.

EDUCATOR: Some frogs like to eat flies.

STUDENT: Yuck!

EDUCATOR: Okay, what you think Fred would like?

STUDENT: How about pizza?

EDUCATOR: What kind?

STUDENT: Maybe pepperoni. How do you spell that?

If possible, keep a running list of memorized chant titles in a prominent location for all to see. Once an exercise is complete, add the title to the list as a way to remind students about the exercise. From time to time, go through the list of titles, and have students recall and perform each chant. During this time, students rehearse a variety of transformations that extend their syntactic repertoires.

Monitoring Progress

Appendix C includes a *Recording Form for Syntactic Structures* for convenience in monitoring a student's performance. A separate recording form may be kept for each student. To use this form, locate the targeted syntactic structure on the form and then record the date the chant exercise was used, the number of the selected chant exercise, and note the performance level of the student. The following codes can be used:

FD—Full dependence on adult model for successful sentence combining

ES—Independent chant problem solving with extensive support from adult

MS—Independent chant problem solving with minimal support from adult

I—Independent chant problem solving

FP—Independent chant problem solving and full participation in oral/choral chanting using title or picture cue only

Figure 4 presents an example of a partially completed recording form.

Recording Form for Syntactic Structures

Student Name: _____*Carla L.*_____

Indicate the date, chant number, and student's level of performance for the chant exercise in the columns to the right of the syntactic structure. Use the following scale for level of performance:

FD— *Full dependence* on adult model for successful sentence combining

ES— Independent chant problem solving with *extensive support* from adult

MS— Independent chant problem solving with *minimal support* from adult

I— *Independent* chant problem solving

FP— Independent chant problem solving and *full participation* in oral/choral chanting using title or picture cue only

Phrase Coordination					
Adjective					
and	1/9, #53-ES	2/4, #72-MS			
but					
or					
Noun					
and					
and + SV*					
but	1/16, #80-MS				
or					
Verb					
and	1/9, #53-ES	2/12, #87-MS			
but	1/16, #80-MS	2/12, #87-MS			
or					
then					

Figure 4 Example of a *Partially Completed* Recording Form for Syntactic Structures

Chapter 2
Phonological Awareness

Recently, as we sat down for a light dinner, our granddaughter (age three) tumbled out of her chair, then looked up and said with obvious embarrassment, "Why are some of us *in* chairs?" Her wide-eyed question prompted amusement around the table. Later, at the same meal, our son urged her to eat her potatoes. When she kept asking, "Why?" he finally said, with exasperation, "Because I like to *argue*, Tori." Her reply was "Don't *arg me*, Daddy!"

This story emphasizes that three-year-olds who are developing normally can understand and produce spoken language with remarkable ease and facility. Tori's steadily developing oral language is the foundation for her already emerging literacy. Although she may have little explicit awareness of the structure of language, her tacit knowledge of phonology and grammar seems highly developed. For example, in segmenting *argue* into two words—*arg* and *you*—her response to her dad makes perfect phonological and syntactic sense.

With support, encouragement, and maturation, Tori's tacit knowledge of language will not only become more accurate but also more explicit. In other words, with literacy instruction, she will come to "know what she knows." The focus of this chapter is phonological awareness—helping learners only a little older than Tori develop their facility with the sound structure of our language. The development of such knowledge, rooted firmly in oral language practice, is critical for subsequent literacy success.

Language Acquisition Revisited

It is assumed that children with intact neurological systems learn to talk in much the same way they learn to walk, ride a bike, or jump curbs with a skateboard: they figure it out for themselves. Adults and peers provide support, but children learn meaningful tasks through interaction with the social situation as well as through individual effort. Just as children do not learn to ride bikes by studying separate skills of pedaling, steering, balancing, and braking, they do not learn phonology or syntax by studying bits and pieces of language. Phonological awareness is a byproduct of language events that the child regards as meaningful.

Three conditions must exist as children learn language. First, the child must *want* to learn. In other words, the child must see talking (or writing) as a useful, interesting, and socially valued activity (like walking, bike riding, or skateboarding). Second, the child must have abundant opportunities to practice in meaningful ways. After all, no one learns a new skill by not doing it. And third, the child must make mistakes so as to receive feedback. Miscues of various kinds, like Tori's segmenting of *argue* into two independent morphemes, provide teachers and learners with vital information for improving performance over time. Children are short-changed if their language education fails to integrate motivation, practice, and feedback.

How do these principles relate to chanting activities and the development of phonological awareness? Consider these points. The fact that most children like rhythmic, rhyming language (chants, nursery rhymes, and songs) is important for student motivation. As far as children are concerned, not only do rhymes often give rise to funny stories, but they are frequently embedded in pleasurable read-aloud activities. In addition, the very nature of chants suggests that they are repeated and internalized. Chants are practiced orally (since speech is our primary language system), with writing coming at a later stage as inner speech is transcribed. Finally, feedback occurs as the learner hears and begins to use new words and syntax with the support of peers, teachers, and family members.

Chants, however, are only an adjunct to a curriculum of language education. These exercises are gentle nudges toward metaphonological knowledge. In remembering this point, do not expect instant results from sentence-combining exercises or other activities for developing phonological awareness. Mastery of such skills takes time, patience, and consistency in teaching practices.

Phonological Awareness Defined

Today, because of the ongoing debate about "phonics" versus "whole language" instruction in reading, many teachers and speech-language professionals are nervous about terms like *phonological awareness*. Does using this term put us in one ideological camp or the other, they ask. We don't think so. In fact, none of the teachers we know espouse "drill-and-kill" instruction, though many value phonics. In addition, none believe in pointless, "whatever-feels-good" activities, though many value meaningful literature-based teaching.

In 1998, the Board of Directors of the International Reading Association (IRA) published a position statement in which they clarified three essential and sometimes confusing terms: *phonemic awareness*, *phonological awareness*, and *phonics knowledge*. *Phonemic awareness* is defined as the conscious awareness of the sounds that make up speech ("IRA Board," 1998).

Children who have acquired phonemic awareness can, for example, identify the sounds in the spoken word *frog* (phoneme segmentation); count the number of sounds in the spoken word *frog* (phoneme counting); explain that if you take the first sound from *frog*, you have *rog* (phoneme deletion); or produce the word *frog* from a series of separate given sounds, as in *f–r–o–g* (phoneme blending).

In contrast, *phonological awareness* encompasses phonemic awareness but also includes the conscious awareness of spoken syllables, *rime onsets* (initial consonants or consonant clusters), and *rimes* (the remainder of a word or syllable) ("IRA Board," 1998). Phonological awareness is acquired through children's sound play, syllable and word segmentation, and rhyming.

Finally, *phonics knowledge* involves "knowing the relationship between specific, printed letters (including combinations of letters) and specific, spoken sounds" ("IRA Board," 1998, p. 26). Phonics knowledge includes, for example, knowing that the word *frog* begins with the letter *f*.

The IRA board favors the term *phonemic awareness* because of its more frequent use in the professional literature related to reading and because many researchers have focused specifically on the phoneme (rather than syllables and rhymes) ("IRA Board," 1998). However, in *Strong Rhythms and Rhymes*, the broader, more inclusive term *phonological awareness* is used. As noted above, phonological awareness encompasses phonemic awareness and is developed through word play, rhymes, and segmentation.

Phonological Awareness Development

Typically, preschoolers demonstrate sound awareness when they play with sounds (as in chanting "Fred is a frog that *frumps* on the *fred*"), clap for each syllable in a long name (as in "Cin–der–el–la"), jump rope to the words of a rap, or make up strings of rhyming words and nonsense words (as in *Fred, bed, head, dead, ked, gled, shmed*). Sentence-combining chants provide the instructional occasion for making tacit knowledge about phonology more explicit. In this way, students are assisted toward literacy.

When children enter school, an essential task for beginning reading is to learn that written symbols (graphemes) represent spoken sounds (phonemes) (Stone, Merritt, and Cherkes-Julkowski, 1998). For example, children must learn that the written word *frog* represents four different spoken sounds: *f–r–o–g*. For students to decode written symbols, they must acquire some phonological awareness of the sound sequences in spoken words.

More than 15 years of research evidence points to a strong relationship between a child's awareness of the sound structure of words prior to reading instruction and the child's reading acquisition success (Torgesen, Wagner, and Rashotte, 1994). An important finding has been that one of the strongest predictors of reading success may be phoneme segmentation skills (Ball and Blachman, 1988). The development of phonemic awareness progresses along a continuum from larger to smaller sound units—that is, from word segmentation, to syllable segmentation, to onset and rime, to phoneme segmentation (Stone et al., 1998).

Approximately 20 percent of children do not demonstrate phonemic awareness by the middle of first grade ("IRA Board," 1998). This clearly demonstrates the need for school-based screening of students to assess their phonemic awareness skills (Gilbertson and Bramlett, 1998; Majsterek and Ellenwood, 1995). Research findings also indicate that early difficulties with acquiring phonemic awareness persist and hinder later academic performance (Stone et al., 1998). Finally, Stone and colleagues found evidence that phonemic awareness skills can be explicitly taught to nonreaders, that such teaching facilitates reading and spelling, and that the effects of such teaching are long lasting and positive.

When practicing the exercises in *Strong Rhythms and Rhymes*, students engage in word and syllable segmentation as they clap, snap, or tap their fingers and chant with the group. They engage in onset and rime as they solve sentence-combining tasks and predict the words and phrases that will result in rhyming chants. Such sound manipulation helps students become more sensitive to the sound structure of their language.

Finally, students engage in phoneme and syllable segmentation during extension activities when they respond to questions such as the following:

- How many syllables are in the word *jumping?*
- What sound is at the beginning of the word *head?*
- What sound is at the end of the word *Fred?*
- How many sounds are in the word *bed?*
- What words rhyme with *kick?*
- Is *frog* a long word or a short word?
- What letters do we write for the word *fed?*

Be aware that questions such as the final one above require both phonics knowledge and phonemic awareness.

To summarize, phonological awareness is critical to reading success. For children from language-rich environments, such awareness tends to develop naturally, so they enter school with a well-developed repertoire of skills, ready and eager for phonics instruction. For other children, more background work is needed. When phonological awareness is lacking, it can and should be taught both prior to and along with phonics instruction (Adams, Foorman, Lundberg, and Beeler, 1998; Goldsworthy, 1998; McFadden, 1998).

The rhythmic sentence-combining chants in this resource provide a socially supportive, language-rich context for learning and practicing phonological awareness. Students gain syllable and word segmentation skills as they practice a selected chant. In solving sentence-combining tasks and predicting rhyming elements, they use language in ways they find fun and interesting. In extension activities, where students create additional verses or transform language, they practice specific phonemic awareness skills. The *Rhyme Family Index* (see page 274) helps to identify specific rhymes targeted in the chant exercises.

Phonological Awareness in Perspective

Phonological awareness develops in a supportive social context—one in which the tasks of rhyme prediction, rhyme repetition, syllable and word segmentation, and creative extension are the repeated focus of the child's attention. For example, PBS's *Sesame Street* engages preschool children in daily demonstrations of phonological awareness. Similarly, children who "read" memorized Mother Goose rhymes to caregivers are reminders that emergent readers move from the known to the unknown, particularly as they decode text. Thus, although the exercises in this resource assume some minimal reading skills, internalized oral chants may help low-level, struggling readers achieve more literacy success. Clearly, the more spoken and written language are linked, and the more students can participate in such linkage, the stronger literacy learning becomes.

Phonological Awareness Assessment

Phonological awareness can be assessed through formal tests, informal tasks, and observations. The procedure used depends upon the purpose of the assessment.

Formal assessment of phonological awareness skills depends upon norm-referenced and criterion-referenced tests. Such testing procedures are often considered contrived or unnatural, sometimes producing "artificial" results. However, formal assessment measures also have advantages because their results can compare a student to others at the same age or developmental level. This information is important when the desired outcome of assessment is to determine eligibility for services. Finally, formal testing procedures help establish a baseline to document growth in specified areas. Various measures for phonological awareness include the following:

Lindamood Auditory Conceptualization Test (1971) by C. Lindamood and P. Lindamood, Austin, TX: Pro-Ed.

Test of Awareness of Language Segments (1987) by D.J. Sawyer, Austin, TX: Pro-Ed.

Test of Phonological Awareness (1994) by J.K. Torgesen and B.R. Bryant, Austin, TX: Pro-Ed.

To obtain a fuller picture of a student's skills, consider using informal tasks and observations. Most students are happy to have their voices recorded on audiotape or videotape as part of a meaningful class activity. For example, a taped show-and-tell activity, book discussion, or dramatic skit for friends and parents can yield valuable data regarding actual language performance. Children can be asked to perform a recently learned chant and to answer extension questions pertaining to phonological elements of the chant (e.g., "What word rhymes with _____?" "How many sounds were in that word?" "What letter does the word _____ start with?"). Try developing personalized forms and protocols for conducting such informal assessments and observations. These procedures allow relevant information pertaining to phonological awareness to be obtained in a natural, playlike setting. Informal assessment also establishes baseline data and helps document progress.

In general, effective assessment is a byproduct of good teaching, not a decontexualized activity. While word lists, sentence-imitation tasks, cloze procedures, and comprehension questions have their place, there is no better substitute than informed and thoughtful observation of students in natural language settings.

Experiment with a variety of routines and schedules for developing phonological awareness. Pay attention to the level of engagement demonstrated by students in these activities. Use rhyming narrative poems as part of a read-aloud program, and encourage families to do the same. Make "word families" to put up on bulletin boards or walls. Phonological awareness has many different facets, each waiting to be explored.

Chapter 3

A Developmental Ladder of Syntax

Any parent who saves scraps of children's writing cannot help but recognize developmental changes over time. For us, the "and...and...and" sentences produced in the early grades by our children, Kristin and Eric, were cause for applause, not cause for alarm. In the past few years, both have written superb master's theses in their respective fields, with syntax appropriate to the occasion. Looking back, we realize that it was love, patience, and praise that nudged them up the developmental ladder.

Acquiring syntax is a complex task for children. This chapter focuses on the idea of a developmental ladder of syntax. The "ladder" metaphor greatly oversimplifies matters, implying a step-by-step movement from one level (or skill) to the next. The reality of acquisition is far more complex. Children actually work on many skills, or transformations, simultaneously. Moreover, children often regress temporarily as they test out new transformations.

This chapter focuses on broad, developmental outlines and introduces key assumptions related to sentence combining. George Hillocks' *Research on Written Composition: New Directions in Teaching* (1986) and William Strong's *Creative Approaches to Sentence Combining* (1986) both document research on sentence combining, particularly in relation to writing. Both sources are cited in full in the references and are available from the National Council of Teachers of English, Urbana, Illinois 61801, at 217–328–3870. The main findings of Hillocks' and Strong's reports are these:

1. There is strong evidence that sentence combining promotes gain in the ease of sentence construction (syntactic fluency) and movement up the developmental ladder (maturity).

2. There is moderate support for the hypothesis that sentence-combining practice transfers to the real writing of children, enabling them to produce better prose (as experienced teachers judge "better" in scientific studies).

3. There is mixed support for the proposition that sentence combining improves reading comprehension (Combs, 1977; Hillocks, 1986; Hunt, 1977; Strong, 1986; Wilkinson and Patty, 1993).

By integrating lively sentence-combining exercises into a language curriculum on a regular basis, students should experience more-than-normal syntax development over time. Other linguistic benefits may also accrue, though these effects seem less certain. When done appropriately, sentence-combining practice is worth doing.

A Perspective on Syntax

Our basic position can be simply stated: *children internalize language in all its rich complexity through abundant and meaningful opportunities for listening, speaking, reading, and writing.* Now, to sharpen that perspective, reconsider the italicized sentence above. Here are its essential ideas, the underlying "kernel" sentences:

- Children internalize language.

- The internalization has complexity.

- The complexity is rich.

- The internalization is through opportunities.

- The opportunities are abundant.

- The opportunities are meaningful.

- The opportunities are for listening.

- The opportunities are for speaking.

- The opportunities are for reading.

- The opportunities are for writing.

According to the theory of transformational/generative grammar, sentences such as these make up the *deep structure* (or underlying meaning) for the *surface structure* expressed earlier (i.e., the italicized position statement). Many surface structures can be derived from the same underlying ideas, depending on how the kernel sentences are combined.

Transformational theory suggests that children gradually acquire the rules for increasingly mature syntax through the activities of listening, speaking, reading, and writing. As in vocabulary acquisition, children understand far more at first than they themselves can actually produce. Over time, however, their ability to use what they have tacitly learned begins to assert itself, slowly but surely. This development—a movement up the ladder of syntax—is enhanced in language-rich environments.

The facts of syntax development, based on the research of Hunt (1965, 1977) and O'Donnell, Griffin, and Norris (1967), point to increasing complexity as children grow older. More specifically, features such as increased clause length, depth of modification, and nominalization seem to characterize developing maturity in syntax. Summarizing Hunt's research, Moffett (1992) described the key features of sentence growth by concluding that there is

> (1) increasing modification of nouns by large clusters of adjectives, relative clauses, and reduced relative clauses; (2) increasing use of nominalization other than nouns and pronouns for subjects and objects (clauses, infinitival and gerundive constructions); and (3) embedding of sentences to an increasing depth (entailed by 1 and 2). (p. 50)

Loban (1976) confirmed the validity of this view in a longitudinal study of language development with students in kindergarten through 12th grade. According to Loban, less-successful writers were constrained not so much by deficits of vocabulary or intelligence as by syntactic shackles. Conversely, students who experienced success with language were able to manipulate phrases and sentence parts to achieve their aims. Similarly, Moffett (1992) contended that "to be *able* to reduce clauses and embed them in each other…indicates fairly advanced growth [but that] complexity for its own sake is no mark of maturity" (pp. 48–49). Moffett's position—a cornerstone for what follows—is that "complexity [in syntax] is necessary but not sufficient for fullest growth [of the speaker or writer]" (p. 49).

Syntax Development in Oral Language

Drawing upon the work of Scott (1988a, 1988b), several key findings from the research on students' oral language development deserve mention. Syntax development can be described in terms of clause-level elaboration and phrase-level elaboration. First consider the use of clauses.

Table 1	Coordination in Oral Language Development
Preschool and Early Elementary	*Mid-Elementary and Above*
and is dominant coordinator *but* increases in frequency *or* usage is rare	*and* usage continues but decreases in frequency other connectors emerge

Clause Level—Clauses are added to sentences by either *coordination* or *subordination*. In coordination, clauses are added by linking; that is, clauses are related semantically and share equal status.

Key developmental facts regarding clauses used for coordination (Scott, 1988b) are summarized in Table 1 on page 31. In subordination, clauses are added by embedding one clause within a main clause. Subordinate clauses may contain either finite verbs (the element of the verb phrase with present or past tense) or nonfinite verbs (infinitives, *-ing* participles, and *-ed* participles).

Table 2	**Subordination in Oral Language Development**
Adverbial Clauses	
Preschool and Early Elementary	*Mid-Elementary and Above*
Time *(when)* and reason *(because)* clauses predominate. Initially, time subordinators correspond to actual temporal sequence. *If, [in order] to,* and *so [that]* increase in conversation. Other subordinators occur rarely. Examples: • *The dog moved <u>so he could catch the frog</u>.* • *He yelled <u>to try to stop the frog</u>.*	Expanded meanings include concession *(though, even, if, unless)* and manner *(as).* Repertoire increases as discourse types expand. Nonfinite forms occur but are more typical in writing. Examples: • *I will feed the frog <u>even though he just ate</u>.* • *He got mad at the frog <u>for hopping on his head</u>.*
Nominal Clauses	
Preschool and Early Elementary	*Mid-Elementary and Above*
Infinitive-as-object has high frequency. *That* and *wh-* nominals emerge—used first with *say, know,* and *think,* then later with a variety of main-clause verbs. Examples: • *The frog wants <u>to hop</u>.* • *I know <u>where the frog is</u>.*	Nonfinite nominals and nominals-as-subjects characterize development. Examples: • *The boy could see <u>the frog hopping</u>.* • *<u>Hopping on the boy's head</u> is funny.*
Relative Clauses	
Preschool and Early Elementary	*Mid-Elementary and Above*
Clauses frequently appear in the predicate of sentences; *that* and *what* are common pronouns; *who* and *where* also begin to emerge. Examples: • *He found the frog in the cage <u>where he had left him</u>.* • *Fred was the frog <u>that was hopping on his head</u>.*	Other pronouns *(whose, which, in which)* appear. These sometimes modify the subject. Nonfinite and nonrestrictive forms may appear. Examples: • *He did a trick, <u>which was slick</u>.* • *Another, <u>crouched nearby</u>, didn't hop on my head.*

Findings for clause subordination are more complex. On average, 2 to 3 out of every 10 sentences spoken by nine-year-olds will contain a subordinate clause (Scott, 1988b). Over 90 percent of all subordination will be one of three major clause types—adverbial, nominal, or relative. Adverbial and nominal clauses account for 80 percent of the subordination; relative clauses, in particular, signal developing maturity in syntax. Ratios of subordinate clauses in spoken and written language differ little when discourse type is controlled (Scott, 1988b). Table 2 summarizes adverbial, nominal, and relative clause subordination development in oral language.

Phrase Level—In spoken language, noun phrase (NP) postmodification by means of prepositional phrases increases throughout the school years. Usually the NP expansions occur as post-verbal elements. Active growth is demonstrated for the following italicized structures in particular:

Prepositional Phrases: "He has a frog *on his head.*"
Appositives: "It's about Fred, *a frog.*"

Phrase structures like the ones above are actually reduced clauses. The prepositional phrase is reduced from "that is on his head." Similarly, the appositive is a reduced relative clause ("who is a frog"). Children begin using phrases as their language becomes more refined and precise. The addition of phrases into a child's repertoire is often an indication of increased language complexity. Longer clauses are replaced with phrases so that a message may be relayed in a more mature and succinct fashion.

Syntax Development in Written Language

From the overview of oral syntax established in the preceding section, let's turn to a series of developmental guidelines derived from research in written language. Joseph Lawlor's (1983) work, *Sentence Combining: A Sequence for Instruction,* is particularly noteworthy. Lawlor's review of many sentence combining studies led him to assert that "we have every reason to believe that sentence combining can play a useful role in composition instruction" (p. 55).

According to Lawlor, "the process of acquiring syntax takes place over a longer period of time than we once thought" (p. 56). In addition, certain syntactic structures are used more often in written form, which disadvantages students with limited reading experience. Finally, students whose native language is not English do not bring the same oral language facility to instruction that native speakers do. Concluding that sentence combining may indeed teach new skills to students, Lawlor set forth a series of research-based developmental sequences that have been adapted as frameworks for *Strong Rhythms and Rhymes.*

What are the broad, developmental trends of written syntax acquisition that educators should understand? Lawlor provided an overview:

First, language users develop basic sentences before they learn to elaborate on these sentences. When elaborations do appear, they occur first in the predicate phrase. For example, students will generally use relative clauses to modify direct objects before they use such clauses to modify subject nouns. Consequently, it makes sense to introduce sentence-combining operations in the predicate phrase first before introducing them in other sentence positions.

Second, there is a general tendency to elaborate with full clauses first, followed by phrases and words that are derived from full clauses. This suggests that relative clauses should be sequenced before reduced clausal structures such as participial phrases and appositives. (p. 56)

With Lawlor's research-based developmental sequences as background, four tables have been created to organize a developmental ladder of written syntax. Tables 3–6 will help users understand and use the *Syntactic Structures Index.*

Strong Rhythms and Rhymes deals mainly with the first two levels of each developmental sequence listed in each table. However, in the case of Table 6 (*Sequence for Noun Substitutes*), most of this resource's attention is focused at Level 1. Also, Lawlor's sequence for free modifiers has been excluded since those structures typically develop quite late—and, for some students, not at all. *Strong Rhythms and Rhymes* focuses on critical syntactic structures that develop during the elementary school years.

While Lawlor's levels are very useful as a "window" on syntax development, professional judgment must be exercised when selecting chants. Work in sentence combining can be easy or difficult for many reasons, and syntax development is only one of them. Vocabulary, content familiarity, and level of abstraction all may affect students' comprehension and motivation. Generally, Lawlor's three levels have been used as a point of departure for classifying chants as *easy, moderate,* or *difficult.* However, a number of factors beyond syntax were considered when rating each chant exercise. The designations of *easy, moderate,* and *difficult* should not be directly equated to Lawlor's three levels of developmental syntax, because what is easy for one student may be difficult for another.

When choosing exercises, begin with *easy* chants and then gradually move on to *moderate* and *difficult* chants as students seem ready for them. However, remember that motivated students can often handle chants above their developmental level. For example, a lively discussion about camping trips might prompt selection of *Chant 8: Camping,* which includes moderately difficult work on the *because of* structure in a phrase. With cues and support, students could probably handle the level 3 (phrase) structure "Camp is fun because of bugs" before dealing with the level 2 (clause) structure in another chant. Educators must weigh multiple factors when selecting materials.

Table 3	**Sequence for Coordinate Structures**

Level 1

Compound sentences
Fred was a frog, and he belonged to me.

Compound structures within the predicate phrase
Fred ate pizza and French fries.
Fred jumped on the bed and landed on me.
Fred was green and friendly.

Compound subjects
Fred and I slept upstairs.

Level 2

Compound prenominal adjectives
The playful and hungry frog liked to jump high.

Level 3

Compound objects of prepositions and verbals
Fred often hopped in the sink and on the counter.
Fred wanted to visit my pals and my school.

Table 3 provides a sequence for coordinate structures. Note, for example, that the coordination of adjectives develops much later than noun coordination or verb coordination. In general, students work from clausal coordination (compound sentences) to phrasal coordination (compound structures at the word or phrase level).

Table 4 on page 36 presents the sequence for adverbial structures, including adverb embedding (single-word adverbs), prepositional phrases, and adverb clauses of various types. As noted earlier, complete clauses gradually give way to reduced clauses or phrase structures.

Table 5 on page 37 presents a number of fine distinctions in the sequence for restrictive noun modifiers. Level 1 structures appear in the predicate, whereas Level 2 structures are embedded as subject modifiers. For most elementary students, Level 1 is clearly easier than Level 2. Adjectival prepositional phrases (Level 2) are actually reduced relative clauses; as such, they represent a movement up the developmental ladder. To use such a structure is to say more in fewer words—a hallmark of developing maturity.

Table 4	Sequence for Adverbial Structures
	Level 1
	Single-word adverbs
	In my class, the frog leaped up <u>quickly</u>.
	Prepositional phrases of place/motion
	He had once again landed <u>on my head</u>.
	Adverb clauses of time—clause order matches time order
	He fell <u>before I could move</u>.
	Adverb clauses of reason—result stated before reason
	Fred ate the fly <u>because he was hungry</u>.
	Level 2
	Adverb clauses of time—clause order does not match time order
	We went outside <u>after I fed him</u>.
	Adverb clauses of reason—reason stated before result
	<u>Because the frog was sleepy</u>, he took a nap.
	Prepositional phrases of time
	I took Fred home with me <u>on Friday afternoon</u>.
	Adverb clauses of condition
	Dad threatened to buy a snake <u>if Fred doesn't behave</u>.
	Adverbial infinitives
	I am waiting <u>to hear more from Mom about this</u>.
	Level 3
	Prepositional phrases of cause, manner, and concession
	The house was quiet <u>because of Fred's absence</u>.
	Then I heard Fred croak <u>with a hungry voice</u>.
	I decided to let him in, <u>despite his mischief</u>.
	Adverb clauses of concession and purpose
	<u>Although Fred came back</u>, he didn't look well.
	I kissed the frog <u>so that he wouldn't be sad</u>.

Table 5	**Sequence for Restrictive Noun Modifiers**

Level 1

Single-word prenominal adjectives
Fred had a <u>sick</u> look.

Relative clauses modifying object—relative pronoun as subject
He was a frog <u>who needed attention</u>.

Relative clauses modifying object—relative pronoun as object
Fred ignored the pizza <u>that I gave him</u>.

Relative clauses modifying object—relative pronoun as possessive
I smiled at the frog <u>whose antics often amused me</u>.

Level 2

Relative pronoun modifying subject—relative pronoun as subject
Frogs <u>that eat pizza</u> sometimes get indigestion.

Relative pronoun modifying subject—relative pronoun as object
The pizza <u>that Fred ate</u> had pepperoni on it.

Relative pronoun modifying subject—relative pronoun as possessive
The frog <u>whose attitude was improving</u> smiled back at me.

Adjectival prepositional phrases
Unfortunately, a wart <u>on my lip</u> looked rather unsightly.

Postnominal participial phrases—past and present
Fred was a frog <u>trying to kiss me again</u>.
I looked at the pizza <u>made for Fred alone</u>.

Restrictive appositive
Finally, I kissed my frog <u>Fred</u>.

Null-pronoun [signaled in brackets] relative clauses
Dad listened to the story [that] <u>I told</u>.

Postnominal infinitive phrases
He had no reason <u>to doubt my story</u>.

Level 3

Prenominal participles—present and past
The <u>croaking</u> frog had kept him awake all night.
Dad finished off the <u>half-eaten</u> pizza.

Table 6	Sequence for Noun Substitutes

Level 1

Factive noun clauses as direct objects
> Mom said [that] Fred was a pest.

Interrogative noun clauses as direct objects
> She knew where he liked to hide out.

Level 2

Factive and interrogative noun clauses as subjects
> [The fact] that she kicked him outdoors bothered us.
> How Fred helped other frogs get in was a mystery to her.

Infinitive phrases
> Mom wanted to order frog legs in a restaurant.
> [For her] to do that would have been unkind to Fred.

Wh-word + infinitive phrase
> Mom finally learned how to get along with the frog.
> Where to put Fred's family then became her problem.

Level 3

Factive and interrogative noun clauses as objects of verbals and prepositions
> Mom needed to know what Fred had in mind.
> Despite the fact that he had a boy's name, Fred was a girl frog.

Gerunds and gerund phrases
> Fred's family loves swimming.
> Raising a frog family now keeps me very busy.

It extraposition with noun clauses, infinitives, and gerunds
> It surprised me that Fred was actually a girl frog.
> It took me a while to call the frog "her."
> It was fun seeing Fred's swimming lessons.

Derived nouns and noun phrases
> Frog abuse can no longer be condoned.
> We need to protest society's insensitivity to Frog Rights.

Table 6 contains the developmental sequence for noun substitutes. Several noun clause structures, many of which are characteristic of mature syntax, are described. While *Strong Rhythms and Rhymes* provides some practice with noun clauses, the focus is primarily on structures that students are likely to use more often in their discourse. Such frequently occurring transformations, like the restrictive appositive shown in Table 5, Level 2 (see page 37), are important for students to understand and practice.

Checking back to Tables 3–6 might be necessary and important when assessing a student's syntax, when planning goals and objectives, and when first using the *Syntactic Structures Index*. Over time, as the sequence of syntax development becomes more familiar, it will be less necessary to refer to the charts.

Syntax Assessment

Assessing syntax from time to time is essential. For such analysis, a sampling of syntactic progress for each student should occur at least once a month. Of course, for many students, periodic data collection regarding syntax development will be a required component of a specialized educational program or an individualized educational program (IEP). In addition, for these same students, initial evaluation covering all areas of language development will be required.

Tables 3–6 provide a conceptual tool for informally analyzing what students say or write. Supplementing these tables are formal tests of syntax and other informal assessment procedures. The purpose of language assessment determines the type of procedure used.

Formal assessment of syntax skills can be conducted with norm-referenced and criterion-referenced tests. As with the formal measures discussed in Chapter 2 for phonological awareness, tests of syntax present similar weaknesses (e.g., contrived format and activities). However, such tests can be important when testing a child for the sake of determining eligibility for services. Using formal testing procedures also helps establish a baseline to document growth in specified areas. The degree of validity and reliability varies depending on the test. Formal assessment measures for syntax include the following tests and/or portions of these tests:

> *Test for Auditory Comprehension of Language* (Rev. ed.) (1985) by E. Carrow-Woolfolk, Austin, TX: Pro-Ed.
>
> *Test of Language Development—Intermediate* (3rd ed.) (1997) by D.D. Hammill and P.L. Newcomer, Austin, TX: Pro-Ed.
>
> *Test of Language Development—Primary* (3rd ed.) (1997) by P.L. Newcomer and D.D. Hammill, Austin, TX: Pro-Ed.

Of course, as with measures of phonological awareness, it is inappropriate to use only formal tests to assess syntax skills. Informal procedures, language sampling, and observation allow relevant information pertaining to syntax understanding and use to be obtained in a natural, playlike setting. Such language-sampling procedures can be used to collect baseline data and document progress of syntax skills. In addition, these procedures all allow a child's performance to be compared to developmental data regarding syntax use. These procedures include the following:

> *Developmental Sentence Analysis* (1974) by L. Lee, Evanston, IL: Northwestern University Press.

> *Guide to Analysis of Language Transcripts* (2nd ed.) (1993) by K. Retherford, Eau Claire, WI: Thinking Publications.

> *SALT: A Computer Program for the Systematic Analysis of Language Transcripts* (1991) by J. Miller and R. Chapman, Madison, WI: Language Analysis Laboratory, Waisman Center, University of Wisconsin.

> *Strong Narrative Assessment Procedure* (SNAP) (1998) by C. Strong, Eau Claire, WI: Thinking Publications.

The recommended approach combines formal testing procedures, informal observations, and language sampling so that sentence-combining exercises serve developmental ends. Authentic observations and language sampling can result in relevant and individualized long-term goals and short-term objectives for each student. (Example goals and objectives for syntax are listed in Appendix B.)

A recording form for syntactic structures appears in Appendix C. All syntactic structures included in the sentence-combining chants can be found in the left-hand column. Use of this recording form to document syntax development is explained on pages 20–21.

Part II
Chant Exercises

Chant 1: Back Flip   Level = M

Chant Model

You can learn a new back flip.
Just don't trip or lose your grip.
If you do, your pants will rip.
Oh, you can learn a new back flip!

Syntax Goals

Line 1	Adjective embedding *(new)*	Phrase
Line 2	Verb coordination *(or)*	Phrase
Line 3	Subordination (adverbial—*if*)	Clause
Line 4	Adjective embedding *(new)*	Phrase

Rhyme Families

[-ew] *do, new, you*
[-ip] *flip, grip, rip, trip*

Teaching Ideas

Introductory Sharing:	experiences with gymnastics; watching gymnastics on TV; tumbling in gym class
Vocabulary Targets:	*learn, back flip, trip, "lose your grip," rip*
Extension Activity:	Show pictures of gymnasts in action or a videotaped gymnastics competition.

Comments, Observations, and Additional Teaching Ideas

You can learn a back flip.   _____

It is new.   a _____ back flip.

Just don't trip.   _____

Just don't lose your grip.   or _____.

You do.   If _____,

Your pants will rip.   _____.

You can learn a back flip.   Oh, _____

It is new.   _____!

Chant 2: Bad Days   Level = D

Chant Model

There are days when you can't win.
First you slip and bump your chin.
Then you trip, which skins your shin.
Oh, there are days when you can't win!

Syntax Goals

Line 1	Subordination (adverbial—*when*)	Clause
Line 2	Verb coordination *(and)*	Phrase
Line 3	Subordination (relative—*which)*	Clause
Line 4	Subordination (adverbial—*when*)	Clause

Rhyme Families

[-en] *then, when*
[-in] *chin, shin, win, skin(s)*
[-ip] *slip, trip*

Teaching Ideas

Introductory Sharing: days when everything seems to go wrong; feeling clumsy
Vocabulary Targets: "bad days," "can't win," slip, bump, skins, shin
Extension Activity: Read the book *Alexander and the Terrible, Horrible, No Good, Very Bad Day!* (1972) by Judith Viorst, New York: Atheneum.

Comments, Observations, and Additional Teaching Ideas

There are days.   _____

You can't win.   when _____.

First you slip.   _____

You bump your chin.   and _____.

Then you trip.   _____,

This skins your shin.   which _____.

There are days.   Oh, _____

You can't win.   _____!

Chant 3: Bareback Mac   Level = E

Chant Model

Mac rode bareback to his shack.

There he ate a midnight snack.

Then he yawned and hit the sack.

Oh, Mac rode bareback to his shack!

Syntax Goals

Line 1	Preposition embedding *(to)*	Phrase
Line 2	Noun embedding *(midnight)*	Phrase
Line 3	Verb coordination *(and)*	Phrase
Line 4	Preposition embedding *(to)*	Phrase

Rhyme Family

[-ack] *bareback, Mac, sack, shack, snack*

Teaching Ideas

Introductory Sharing: horseback riding; midnight snacks; snacks before bedtime

Vocabulary Targets: rode, bareback, shack, ate, "midnight snack," "hit the sack"

Extension Activity: Show a picture of a person riding a horse bareback and a rider with a saddle; discuss the differences.

Comments, Observations, and Additional Teaching Ideas

Mac rode bareback.   _____

He rode to his shack.   to _____.

There he ate a snack.   _____

It was at midnight.   a _____ snack.

Then he yawned.   _____

He hit the sack.   and _____.

Mac rode bareback.   Oh, _____

He rode to his shack.   _____!

Chant 4: Big Sneeze   Level = M

Chant Model

Feel the breeze behind my sneeze.

It explodes and shakes the trees.

Worst of all, I sneeze in threes.

Oh, feel the breeze behind my sneeze!

Syntax Goals

Line 1	Preposition embedding *(behind)*	Phrase
Line 2	Verb coordination *(and)*	Phrase
Line 3	Adverb embedding *(worst of all)*	Phrase
Line 4	Preposition embedding *(behind)*	Phrase

Rhyme Family

[-ease] *breeze, sneeze, threes, trees*

Teaching Ideas

Introductory Sharing:	sneezing; sneezing etiquette
Vocabulary Targets:	breeze, sneeze, explodes, shakes, "worst of all," threes, behind
Extension Activity:	Read the book *"Stand Back," Said the Elephant, "I'm Going to Sneeze!"* (1971) by Patricia Thomas, New York: Lothrop, Lee and Shepard.

Comments, Observations, and Additional Teaching Ideas

Feel the breeze.	_____
It is behind my sneeze.	behind _____.
It explodes.	_____
It shakes the trees.	and _____.
I sneeze in threes.	Worst _____,
This is worst of all.	_____.
Feel the breeze.	Oh, _____
It is behind my sneeze.	_____!

Chant 5: Blake Snores   Level = M

Chant Model   ### Syntax Goals

How Blake snores until daybreak.	Line 1	Preposition embedding *(until)*	Phrase
Blake's snoring makes my head ache.	Line 2	Possessive embedding *(Blake's)*	Phrase
Rooms with Blake are hard to take.	Line 3	Preposition embedding *(with)*	Phrase
Oh, how Blake snores until daybreak!	Line 4	Preposition embedding *(until)*	Phrase

Rhyme Family

[-ake] *ache, Blake, daybreak, make(s), take*

Teaching Ideas

Introductory Sharing:	snoring sounds; experiences sharing rooms with snorers
Vocabulary Targets:	*snores, until, daybreak,* "head ache," "hard to take"
Extension Activity:	Read the book *Too Much Noise* (1967) by Ann McGovern, New York: Scholastic Book Services.

Comments, Observations, and Additional Teaching Ideas

How Blake snores.   _____

He snores until daybreak.   until _____.

Snoring makes my head ache.   Blake's _____

The snoring is Blake's.   makes _____.

Rooms are hard to take.   Rooms with _____

They are with Blake.   _____.

How Blake snores.   Oh, _____

He snores until daybreak.   _____!

Chant 6: Burgers and Fries　　　　　　Level = M

Chant Model

We love burgers, and we love fries.

These bring flies of giant size.

Flies for supper are a surprise.

Oh, we love burgers, and we love fries!

Syntax Goals

Line 1	Coordination *(and)*	Clause
Line 2	Preposition embedding *(of)*	Phrase
Line 3	Preposition embedding *(for)*	Phrase
Line 4	Coordination *(and)*	Clause

Rhyme Family

[-ize] *flies, fries, size, surprise*

Teaching Ideas

Introductory Sharing:　favorite foods; favorite fast-food restaurants; insects at a cookout

Vocabulary Targets:　*burger, fries, flies, giant size, supper, surprise*

Extension Activity:　Make burgers, fries, and flies from clay or play dough, or cut pictures of them out of magazines. Act out the chant using the objects or pictures as props.

Comments, Observations, and Additional Teaching Ideas

We love burgers.   _____,

We love fries.   and _____.

These bring flies.   These _____

They are giant size.   of _____.

Flies are for supper.   Flies for _____

Flies are a surprise.   _____.

We love burgers.   Oh, _____,

We love fries.   _____!

Chant 7: Cake Hater   Level = D

Chant Model

Jake likes pie, but he hates cake.

He says cake is a mistake.

It tastes dry, which he can't take.

Oh, Jake likes pie, but he hates cake!

Syntax Goals

Line 1	Coordination *(but)*	Clause
Line 2	Subordination (nominal—*[that]*)	Clause
Line 3	Subordination (relative—*which*)	Clause
Line 4	Coordination *(but)*	Clause

Rhyme Families

[-ake] *cake, Jake, mistake, take*

[-y] *dry, pie*

Teaching Ideas

Introductory Sharing: favorite desserts

Vocabulary Targets: pie, hate, cake, mistake, "tastes dry," "can't take"

Extension Activity: Ask how many students prefer pie and how many prefer cake. Make a chart showing the results of the "survey." Talk about the results.

Comments, Observations, and Additional Teaching Ideas

Jake likes pie.   _____,

He hates cake.   but _____.

He says something.   _____ cake

Cake is a mistake.   _____.

It tastes dry.   _____,

He can't take it.   which _____.

Jake likes pie.   Oh, _____,

He hates cake.   _____!

Chant 8: Camping   Level = M

Chant Model

Camp is fun because of bugs.

They swim in the water jugs.

Best of all, there are green slugs.

Oh, camp is fun because of bugs!

Syntax Goals

Line 1	Preposition embedding *(because of)*	Phrase
Line 2	Noun embedding *(water)*	Phrase
Line 3	Adverb embedding *(best of all)*	Phrase
Line 4	Preposition embedding *(because of)*	Phrase

Rhyme Family

[-ugs] *bugs, jugs, slugs*

Teaching Ideas

Introductory Sharing: summer camp experiences; catching and collecting bugs

Vocabulary Targets: *camp, water jugs, green slugs*

Extension Activity: Show a picture of a slug or bring in a real one; discuss its habitat and diet.

Comments, Observations, and Additional Teaching Ideas

Camp is fun.   _____

This is because of bugs.   because_____.

They swim in the jugs.   _____

The jugs are for water.   the _____ jugs.

Something is best of all.   Best _____,

There are green slugs.   _____.

Camp is fun.   Oh, _____

This is because of bugs.   _____!

Chant 9: Chanting   Level = E

Chant Model

I love chanting line by line.

When I chant, I feel so fine.

I take chants and make them mine.

Oh, I love chanting line by line!

Syntax Goals

Line 1	Adverb embedding *(line by line)*	Phrase
Line 2	Subordination (adverbial—*when*)	Clause
Line 3	Verb coordination *(and)*	Phrase
Line 4	Adverb embedding *(line by line)*	Phrase

Rhyme Families

[-ake] *make, take*

[-ine] *fine, line, mine*

[-ow] *oh, so*

Teaching Ideas

Introductory Sharing: compare and contrast chanting, rapping, and singing

Vocabulary Targets: *chant, "line by line," "feel so fine," "make them mine"*

Extension Activity: Have the children share chants that are commonly performed on the playground.

Comments, Observations, and Additional Teaching Ideas

I love chanting.

_____

I chant line by line.

line _____.

I chant.

When _____,

I feel so fine.

_____.

I take chants.

_____

I make them mine.

and _____.

I love chanting.

Oh, _____

I chant line by line.

_____!

Chant 10: Chuck's Truck   Level = M

Chant Model

My friend Chuck is out of luck.

He just crashed his pickup truck.

It is stuck in knee-deep muck.

Oh, my friend Chuck is out of luck!

Syntax Goals

Line 1	Appositive noun embedding *(Chuck)*	Phrase
Line 2	Noun embedding *(pickup)*	Phrase
Line 3	Adjective embedding *(knee-deep)*	Phrase
Line 4	Appositive noun embedding *(Chuck)*	Phrase

Rhyme Family

[-uck] *Chuck, luck, muck, stuck, truck*

Teaching Ideas

Introductory Sharing:	automobile accidents; experiences with being stuck in the mud
Vocabulary Targets:	"out of luck," crash, pickup truck, stuck, "knee-deep," muck
Extension Activity:	Read the book *Mrs. Wishy Washy* (1998) by Joy Cowley, Bothell, WA: Wright Group.

Comments, Observations, and Additional Teaching Ideas

My friend is out of luck.

My friend Chuck _____

His name is Chuck.

_____.

He just crashed his truck.

_____

His truck is a pickup.

his _____ truck.

It is stuck in muck.

_____

The muck is knee-deep.

in _____ muck.

My friend is out of luck.

Oh, _____

His name is Chuck.

_____!

Chant 11: Cool Cat   Level = D

Chant Model

On Matt's head is a ratty hat.

His style and smile show where it's at.

Some call him cool, while some
    call him cat.

Oh, on Matt's head is a ratty hat!

Syntax Goals

Line 1	Adjective embedding *(ratty)*	Phrase
Line 2	Noun coordination *(and + show)*	Phrase
Line 3	Subordination (adverbial—*while)*	Clause
Line 4	Adjective embedding *(ratty)*	Phrase

Rhyme Families

[-at] *at, cat, hat, Matt, rat(ty)*

[-ile] *smile, style, while*

Teaching Ideas

Introductory Sharing: clothing and accessories for pets; experiences dressing up pets

Vocabulary Targets: *ratty, style, smile, "where it's at," "cool," "cool cat"*

Extension Activity: Show pictures of pets wearing clothing or costumes. Have each student tell or write a creative story about a picture.

Comments, Observations, and Additional Teaching Ideas

On Matt's head is a hat.   _____

The hat is ratty.   a _____ hat.

His style shows where it's at.   His _____

His smile shows where it's at.   show _____.

Some call him cool.   _____,

Some call him cat.   while _____.

On Matt's head is a hat.   Oh, _____

The hat is ratty.   _____!

Chant 12: Count to Ten

Level = D

Chant Model

		Syntax Goals		
When Ben gets mad, he counts to ten.	Line 1	Subordination (adverbial—*when*)	Clause
Ten slow counts can sure help Ben.	Line 2	Adjective embedding *(slow)*	Phrase
If ten won't work, he tries again.	Line 3	Subordination (adverbial—*if*)	Clause
Oh, when Ben gets mad, he counts to ten!	Line 4	Subordination (adverbial—*when*)	Clause

Rhyme Families

[-en] *again, ten, when*

[-ow] *oh, slow*

Teaching Ideas

Introductory Sharing: experiences with being mad at somebody; ways to control anger

Vocabulary Targets: *mad, count, ten, slow, "won't work," "tries again"*

Extension Activity: Discuss the importance of stopping yourself before saying mean words when you're angry. Have students role-play getting mad and then counting to ten to calm down.

Comments, Observations, and Additional Teaching Ideas

Ben gets mad.

He counts to ten.

Ten counts can sure help Ben.

The counts are slow.

Ten won't work.

He tries again.

Ben gets mad.

He counts to ten.

When _____,

_____.

Ten _____ counts

can _____.

If _____,

_____.

Oh, _____,

_____!

Chant 13: Cutoff Jeans   Level = D

Chant Model

Dean and Jean are in their teens.

Let us tell you what this means.

Both are into cutoff jeans.

Oh, Dean and Jean are in their teens!

Syntax Goals

Line 1	Noun coordination		Phrase
	(and + are + their)		
Line 2	Subordination (nominal—*what*)		Clause
Line 3	Adjective embedding *(cutoff)*		Phrase
Line 4	Noun coordination		Phrase
	(and + are + their)		

Rhyme Families

[-ean] *Dean, Jean, jean(s), mean(s), teen(s)*

[-ew] *into, you*

Teaching Ideas

Introductory Sharing:	cutting jeans to make shorts; why kids like jean shorts
Vocabulary Targets:	*teens, both, cutoff jeans*
Extension Activity:	Bring a pair of old jeans to class and have the children help cut them to make shorts.

Comments, Observations, and Additional Teaching Ideas

Dean is in his teens. _____

Jean is in her teens. are _____.

Let us tell you something. _____

This means something. what _____.

Both are into jeans. _____

The jeans are cutoff. into _____ jeans.

Dean is in his teens. Oh, _____

Jean is in her teens. _____!

Chant 14: Dirt Bikes   Level = M

Chant Model

Dirk likes dirt bikes in the hills.
Dirt bikes give him thrills and spills.
His folks get lots of doctor bills.
Oh, Dirk likes dirt bikes in the hills!

Syntax Goals

Line 1	Preposition embedding *(in)*	Phrase
Line 2	Noun coordination *(and)*	Phrase
Line 3	Noun embedding *(doctor)*	Phrase
Line 4	Preposition embedding *(in)*	Phrase

Rhyme Families

[-ikes] *bikes, likes*
[-ills] *bills, hills, spills, thrills*

Teaching Ideas

Introductory Sharing:	experiences riding dirt bikes; places to ride dirt bikes; getting hurt when riding a bike
Vocabulary Targets:	*dirt bikes, hills, thrills, spills, doctor bills, folks*
Extension Activity:	Bring in magazines about dirt bikes or motorcycles to share with the group. Allow students to look through the magazines during free reading time.

Comments, Observations, and Additional Teaching Ideas

Dirk likes dirt bikes. _____

He likes riding them in the hills.　in _____ .

Dirt bikes give him thrills. _____

Dirt bikes give him spills.　_____ and _____ .

His folks get lots of bills. _____

The bills are from the doctor.　lots of _____ bills.

Dirk likes dirt bikes.　Oh, _____

He likes riding them in the hills. _____ !

Chant 15: Dog Bath   Level = M

Chant Model

Bert and Gert smell very foul.

Bathing makes them yowl and howl.

Bert will scowl, and Gert will growl.

Oh, Bert and Gert smell very foul!

Syntax Goals

Line 1	Noun coordination *(and + smell)*	Phrase
Line 2	Verb coordination *(and)*	Phrase
Line 3	Coordination *(and)*	Clause
Line 4	Noun coordination *(and + smell)*	Phrase

Rhyme Families

[-ert] *Bert, Gert*

[-owl] *foul, growl, howl, scowl, yowl*

Teaching Ideas

Introductory Sharing:	taking care of pets; bathing pets
Vocabulary Targets:	*smell, foul, bathing, yowl, howl, scowl, growl*
Extension Activity:	Ask the students to brainstorm pet care suggestions. Write the ideas where everyone can see.

Comments, Observations, and Additional Teaching Ideas

Bert smells very foul.   _____ and _____

Gert smells very foul.   _____.

Bathing makes them yowl.   _____

Bathing makes them howl.   _____ and _____.

Bert will scowl.   _____,

Gert will growl.   and _____.

Bert smells very foul.   Oh, _____

Gert smells very foul.   _____!

Chant 16: Don the Dog   Level = D

Chant Model

Don is a dog that you like to love.

His skin fits him like an old, worn glove.

He croons to the moon,
  which is high above.

Oh, Don is a dog that you like to love!

Syntax Goals

Line 1	Subordination (relative—*that*)	Clause
Line 2	Preposition embedding *(like)*	Phrase
Line 3	Subordination (relative—*which*)	Clause
Line 4	Subordination (relative—*that*)	Clause

Rhyme Families

[-is] *his, is*

[-oon] *croon, moon*

[-ove] *above, glove, love*

Teaching Ideas

Introductory Sharing: dogs as pets; types of dogs; noises dogs make

Vocabulary Targets: *love, skin, fits, "worn glove," croon, moon, "high above," "fits like a glove"*

Extension Activity: Read the book *The Puppy Who Wanted a Boy* (1988) by Jane Thayer, New York: William Morrow.

Comments, Observations, and Additional Teaching Ideas

Don is a dog. _____

You like to love him. that _____.

His skin fits him. _____

It is like an old, worn glove. like _____.

He croons to the moon. _____,

It is high above. which _____.

Don is a dog. Oh, _____

You like to love him. _____!

Chant 17: Dream Team   Level = M

Chant Model

We're a team that has a dream.
After we win, we'll get ice cream.
Then we'll scream and let off steam.
Oh, we're a team that has a dream!

Syntax Goals

Line 1	Subordination (relative—*that*)	Clause
Line 2	Subordination (adverbial—*after*)	Clause
Line 3	Verb coordination *(and)*	Phrase
Line 4	Subordination (relative—*that*)	Clause

Rhyme Families

[-eam] *cream, dream, scream, steam, team*
[-et] *get, let*

Teaching Ideas

Introductory Sharing: experiences playing team sports; celebrating after winning a game
Vocabulary Targets: *team, dream, win, scream, "let off steam"*
Extension Activity: Teach the children a basketball or football cheer. Perform the cheer as a group.

Comments, Observations, and Additional Teaching Ideas

We're a team.   _____

The team has a dream.   that _____.

We win.   After _____,

We'll get ice cream.   _____.

Then we'll scream.   _____

Then we'll let off steam.   and _____.

We're a team.   Oh, _____

The team has a dream.   _____!

Chant 18: Fall Colors   Level = M

Chant Model

Leaves turn bright as nights grow cool.

Workers drain the swimming pool.

Football games are after school.

Oh, leaves turn bright as nights
    grow cool!

Syntax Goals

Line 1	Subordination (adverbial—*as*)	Clause
Line 2	Gerund embedding *(swimming)*	Phrase
Line 3	Adjective embedding *(football)*	Phrase
Line 4	Subordination (adverbial—*as*)	Clause

Rhyme Families

[-ite] *bright, night(s)*

[-ool] *cool, pool, school*

Teaching Ideas

Introductory Sharing: things people do to get ready for winter; signs of fall

Vocabulary Targets: "fall colors," "leaves turn bright," nights, "grow cool," workers, drain, swimming pool, football games

Extension Activity: Have the children bring fall leaves to school and make collages with them.

Comments, Observations, and Additional Teaching Ideas

Leaves turn bright. _____

Nights grow cool. as _____.

Workers drain the pool. _____

The pool is for swimming. the _____ pool.

Games are after school. Football _____

The games are football. _____.

Leaves turn bright. Oh, _____

Nights grow cool. _____!

Chant 19: Floyd the Flea   Level = M

Chant Model

Floyd is a flea you can barely see.
He flits as he sits upon my knee.
Itches make twitches for kids like me.
Oh, Floyd is a flea you can barely see!

Syntax Goals

Line 1	Subordination (relative—*[that]*)	Clause
Line 2	Preposition embedding *(upon)*	Phrase
Line 3	Preposition embedding *(for)*	Phrase
Line 4	Subordination (relative—*[that]*)	Clause

Rhyme Families

[-ee] *flea, knee, me, see*
[-itches] *itches, twitches*
[-its] *flits, sits*

Teaching Ideas

Introductory Sharing: insects; pets with fleas; why fleas make you itch
Vocabulary Targets: *flea, barely, flits, itches, twitches, upon*
Extension Activity: Bring in an animal flea-and-tick collar and explain its use.

Comments, Observations, and Additional Teaching Ideas

Floyd is a flea.   _____

You can barely see him.   you _____.

He flits as he sits.   _____

He sits upon my knee.   upon _____.

Itches make twitches.   _____

These are for kids like me.   for _____.

Floyd is a flea.   Oh, _____

You can barely see him.   _____!

Chant 20: Flying Free   Level = M

Chant Model

We see eagles at the beach.

They fly high beyond our reach.

Flying free is what they teach.

Oh, we see eagles at the beach!

Syntax Goals

Line 1	Preposition embedding *(at)*	Phrase
Line 2	Preposition embedding *(beyond)*	Phrase
Line 3	Adjective embedding *(free)*	Phrase
Line 4	Preposition embedding *(at)*	Phrase

Rhyme Families

[-each] *beach, reach, teach*

[-ee] *free, see, we*

[-y] *fly, high*

Teaching Ideas

Introductory Sharing:	experiences at the beach; seeing eagles in the wild
Vocabulary Targets:	eagles, beach, "fly high," "beyond our reach," "flying free," teach
Extension Activity:	Have the children draw pictures of eagles flying.

Comments, Observations, and Additional Teaching Ideas

We see eagles. _____

They are at the beach. at _____.

They fly high. _____

They are beyond our reach. beyond _____.

Flying is what they teach. Flying _____ is

The flying is free. _____.

We see eagles. Oh, _____

They are at the beach. _____!

Chant 21: Fred the Frog   Level = D

Chant Model

Fred is a frog that jumps on the bed.

With a quick kick, he lands
  on my head.

His trick is slick, so he can get fed.

Oh, Fred is a frog that jumps on the bed!

Syntax Goals

Line 1	Subordination (relative—*that*)	Clause
Line 2	Preposition embedding *(with)*	Phrase
Line 3	Subordination (adverbial—*so [that]*)	Clause
Line 4	Subordination (relative—*that*)	Clause

Rhyme Families

[-ed] *bed, fed, Fred, head*

[-ick] *kick, quick, slick, trick*

[-is] *his, is*

[-ow] *oh, so*

Teaching Ideas

Introductory Sharing:	pets; frogs as pets; pets that do tricks for food
Vocabulary Targets:	*quick kick, trick, "slick," fed*
Extension Activity:	Using a stuffed toy frog, demonstrate hopping, jumping, and landing.

Comments, Observations, and Additional Teaching Ideas

Fred is a frog.　　　　　　＿＿＿＿＿＿＿＿＿＿＿＿＿＿＿＿＿＿＿＿

He jumps on the bed.　　　that ＿＿＿＿＿＿＿＿＿＿＿＿＿＿＿＿.

He makes a quick kick.　　With ＿＿＿＿＿＿＿＿＿＿＿＿＿＿＿＿,

He lands on my head.　　　he ＿＿＿＿＿＿＿＿＿＿＿＿＿＿＿＿＿.

His trick is slick.　　　　＿＿＿＿＿＿＿＿＿＿＿＿＿＿＿＿＿＿,

He can get fed.　　　　　so ＿＿＿＿＿＿＿＿＿＿＿＿＿＿＿＿.

Fred is a frog.　　　　　　Oh, ＿＿＿＿＿＿＿＿＿＿＿＿＿＿＿＿

He jumps on the bed.　　　＿＿＿＿＿＿＿＿＿＿＿＿＿＿＿＿＿＿!

Chant 22: Frosty Toes   Level = D

Chant Model

Lulu lost her bright blue shoe.

Her nose grew cold, and her
    toes did too.

When Lulu got home, she had the flu.

Oh, Lulu lost her bright blue shoe!

Syntax Goals

Line 1	Adjective embedding *(bright blue)*	Phrase
Line 2	Coordination *(and + did)*	Clause
Line 3	Subordination (adverbial—*when*)	Clause
Line 4	Adjective embedding *(bright blue)*	Phrase

Rhyme Families

[-ew] *blue, flu, grew, Lulu, shoe, too*

[-ose] *nose, toes*

Teaching Ideas

Introductory Sharing: how it feels to be cold; what we do to keep warm during winter; how it feels to lose something important

Vocabulary Targets: *lost, bright blue, flu, "grew cold"*

Extension Activity: Brainstorm different kinds of cold weather clothing and write their names where all students can see.

Comments, Observations, and Additional Teaching Ideas

Lulu lost her shoe.   Lulu _____

The shoe was bright blue.   her _____ shoe.

Her nose grew cold.   _____,

Her toes grew cold too.   and _____.

Lulu got home.   When _____,

She had the flu.   _____.

Lulu lost her shoe.   Oh, _____

The shoe was bright blue.   _____!

Chant 23: Ghost Sounds   Level = M

Chant Model

Wind made ghost sounds in the trees.

As we walked, we thought we'd freeze.

We trudged in sludge up to our knees.

Oh, wind made ghost sounds
    in the trees!

Syntax Goals

Line 1	Preposition embedding *(in)*	Phrase
Line 2	Subordination (adverbial—*as*)	Clause
Line 3	Preposition embedding *(up)*	Phrase
Line 4	Preposition embedding *(in)*	Phrase

Rhyme Families

[-ease] *freeze, knees, trees*

[-udge] *sludge, trudge(d)*

Teaching Ideas

Introductory Sharing: ghost stories; experiences with Halloween ghosts; cold and windy weather

Vocabulary Targets: *wind, "ghost sounds," freeze, trudged, sludge*

Extension Activity: Have the children record scary ghost sounds onto audiotape. Play the sounds as background noise while chanting.

Comments, Observations, and Additional Teaching Ideas

Wind made ghost sounds.   _____

The sounds were in the trees.   in _____.

We walked.   As _____,

We thought we'd freeze.   _____.

We trudged in sludge.   _____

It was up to our knees.   up _____.

Wind made ghost sounds.   Oh, _____

The sounds were in the trees.   _____!

Chant 24: Gluey Stew   Level = E

Chant Model

Stew is a food that is good for you.

Put it in milk, and it makes glue.

Feed it to elves, and they turn blue.

Oh, stew is a food that is good for you!

Syntax Goals

Line 1	Subordination (relative—*that*)	Clause
Line 2	Coordination *(and)*	Clause
Line 3	Coordination *(and)*	Clause
Line 4	Subordination (relative—*that*)	Clause

Rhyme Family

[-ew] *blue, glue, stew, to, you*

Teaching Ideas

Introductory Sharing: ingredients for stew; stew recipes

Vocabulary Targets: *stew, glue, feed, elves,* "turn blue," "good for you"

Extension Activity: Bring in cut-up stew ingredients and a crock pot; supervise while the children make a stew. As another option, have each child bring a designated ingredient to add to the stew.

Comments, Observations, and Additional Teaching Ideas

Stew is a food.   _____

It is good for you.   that _____.

Put it in milk.   _____,

It makes glue.   and _____.

Feed it to elves.   _____,

They turn blue.   and _____.

Stew is a food.   Oh, _____

It is good for you.   _____!

Chant 25: Grandpa's Beard   Level = D

Chant Model

I like Gramps because he's weird.

Once a week, we trim his beard.

We both laugh while he gets sheared.

Oh, I like Gramps because he's weird!

Syntax Goals

Line 1	Subordination (adverbial—*because*)	Clause
Line 2	Adverb embedding *(once a week)*	Phrase
Line 3	Subordination (adverbial—*while*)	Clause
Line 4	Subordination (adverbial—*because*)	Clause

Rhyme Families

[-eard] *beard, sheared, weird*

[-ee] *he, we*

Teaching Ideas

Introductory Sharing: grandparents; getting a haircut

Vocabulary Targets: *Gramps, weird, "once a week," trim, beard, both, "gets sheared"*

Extension Activity: Allow the children to role-play trimming each other's hair.

Comments, Observations, and Additional Teaching Ideas

I like Gramps.   _____

He's weird.   because _____.

We trim his beard.   Once _____,

This is once a week.   _____.

We both laugh.   _____

He gets sheared.   while _____.

I like Gramps.   Oh, _____

He's weird.   _____!

Chant 26: Green Teeth   Level = D

Chant Model

We know kids whose teeth are green.

They should brush to get them clean.

Green on teeth should not be seen.

Oh, we know kids

    whose teeth are green!

Syntax Goals

Line 1	Subordination (relative—*whose*)	Clause
Line 2	Infinitive embedding *([in order] to)*	Phrase
Line 3	Preposition embedding *(on)*	Phrase
Line 4	Subordination (relative—*whose*)	Clause

Rhyme Families

[-ean] *clean, green, seen*

[-ee] *be, we*

[-ow] *oh, know*

Teaching Ideas

Introductory Sharing:	dental hygiene practices; why we need to care for our teeth
Vocabulary Targets:	*teeth, green, brush, clean*
Extension Activity:	Discuss and demonstrate proper brushing techniques.

Comments, Observations, and Additional Teaching Ideas

We know kids.   _____

Their teeth are green.   whose _____.

They should brush.   _____

This would get them clean.   to _____.

Green should not be seen.   Green on _____

The green is on the teeth.   _____.

We know kids.   Oh, _____

Their teeth are green.   _____!

Chant 27: Halloween Fun   Level = M

Chant Model

It's a night for tricks or treats.

Ghosts and goblins prowl the street.

Hear them howl at friends they meet.

Oh, it's a night for tricks or treats!

Syntax Goals

Line 1	Noun coordination *(or)*	Phrase
Line 2	Noun coordination *(and)*	Phrase
Line 3	Subordination (relative—*[that]*)	Clause
Line 4	Noun coordination *(or)*	Phrase

Rhyme Families

[-eat] *meet, street, treat(s)*

[-owl] *howl, prowl*

Teaching Ideas

Introductory Sharing:	trick-or-treating; ghost stories
Vocabulary Targets:	*Halloween, "tricks or treats," ghosts, goblins, prowl, howl, meet*
Extension Activity:	Have the group role-play trick-or-treating and provide a small treat for each child.

Comments, Observations, and Additional Teaching Ideas

It's a night for tricks.   _____

It's a night for treats.   _____ or _____.

Ghosts prowl the street.   _____ and _____

Goblins prowl the street.   _____.

Hear them howl at friends.   _____

They meet friends.   _____ meet.

It's a night for tricks.   Oh, _____

It's a night for treats.   _____!

Chant 28: Hear the Night   Level = M

Chant Model

Close your eyes, and hear the night.

Clouds slide past in white moonlight.

Shadows glide as birds take flight.

Oh, close your eyes, and hear the night!

Syntax Goals

Line 1	Coordination *(and)*	Clause
Line 2	Preposition embedding *(in)*	Phrase
Line 3	Subordination (adverbial—*as*)	Clause
Line 4	Coordination *(and)*	Clause

Rhyme Families

[-ide] *glide, slide*

[-ite] *flight, moonlight, night, white*

Teaching Ideas

Introductory Sharing: experiences with taking a walk at night; noises at night

Vocabulary Targets: *"hear the night," slide, moonlight, shadows, glide, "take flight"*

Extension Activity: Have the children draw pictures of things they hear at night.

Comments, Observations, and Additional Teaching Ideas

Close your eyes.

_____,

Hear the night.

and _____.

Clouds slide past.

_____

They are in white moonlight.

in _____.

Shadows glide.

_____

Birds take flight.

as _____.

Close your eyes.

Oh, _____,

Hear the night.

_____!

Chant 29: Hiking   Level = M

Chant Model

We hike trails through rocks and pine.

Raindrops drip, but we feel fine.

Rain is simply wet sunshine.

Oh, we hike trails

through rocks and pine!

Syntax Goals

Line 1	Noun coordination *(and)*	Phrase
Line 2	Coordination *(but)*	Clause
Line 3	Adjective embedding *(wet)*	Phrase
Line 4	Noun coordination *(and)*	Phrase

Rhyme Family

[-ine] *fine, pine, sunshine*

Teaching Ideas

Introductory Sharing: places to hike; hiking clothing and equipment

Vocabulary Targets: *hiking, trails, rocks, pine, raindrops, drip, "feel fine," "wet sunshine"*

Extension Activity: Bring clothing for hiking to class; let the children try on items.

Comments, Observations, and Additional Teaching Ideas

We hike trails through rocks.   _____

We hike trails through pine.   _____ and _____.

Raindrops drip.   _____,

We feel fine.   but _____.

Rain is simply sunshine.   _____

The sunshine is wet.   wet _____.

We hike trails through rocks.   Oh, _____

We hike trails through pine.   _____!

Chant 30: Hockey   Level = M

Chant Model

Hockey is a winter sport.

First you get an icy court.

Then find skaters, tall and short.

Oh, hockey is a winter sport!

Syntax Goals

Line 1	Noun embedding *(winter)*	Phrase
Line 2	Adjective embedding *(icy)*	Phrase
Line 3	Appositive adjective embedding *(tall* and *short)*	Phrase
Line 4	Noun embedding *(winter)*	Phrase

Rhyme Family

[-ort] *court, short, sport*

Teaching Ideas

Introductory Sharing: hockey; where to play hockey; equipment needed for hockey

Vocabulary Targets: *hockey, sport, winter, first, court, icy, skaters, tall, short*

Extension Activity: Show a picture of children playing hockey; discuss the equipment needed. Brainstorm names of winter sports and where each is played.

Comments, Observations, and Additional Teaching Ideas

Hockey is a sport.   _____

It is played in winter.   a _____ sport.

First you get a court.   _____

The court is icy.   an _____ court.

Then find skaters.   _____,

They are tall and short.   _____ and _____.

Hockey is a sport.   Oh, _____

It is played in winter.   _____!

Chant 31: Hopscotch   Level = D

Chant Model

Let's go out to play hopscotch.
You can hop, while I just watch.
If you try, you'll be topnotch.
Oh, let's go out to play hopscotch!

Syntax Goals

Line 1	Infinitive embedding *([in order] to)*	Phrase
Line 2	Subordination (adverbial—*while*)	Clause
Line 3	Subordination (adverbial—*if*)	Clause
Line 4	Infinitive embedding *([in order] to)*	Phrase

Rhyme Families

[-otch] *hopscotch, topnotch, watch*

[-ow] *oh, go*

[-y] *I, try*

Teaching Ideas

Introductory Sharing: how to play hopscotch
Vocabulary Targets: *hopscotch, watch, try, "topnotch"*
Extension Activity: Take the children outside to play hopscotch.

Comments, Observations, and Additional Teaching Ideas

Let's go out.   _____

This is to play hopscotch.   to _____.

You can hop.   _____,

I just watch.   while _____.

You try.   If _____,

You'll be topnotch.   _____.

Let's go out.   Oh, _____

This is to play hopscotch.   _____!

Chant 32: Hot Dogs   Level = M

Chant Model

Hot dogs play in cold snow banks.

They like chili on their franks.

They get these, and they bark, "Thanks!"

Oh, hot dogs play in cold snow banks!

Syntax Goals

Line 1	Adjective embedding *(cold)*	Phrase
Line 2	Preposition embedding *(on)*	Phrase
Line 3	Coordination *(and)*	Clause
Line 4	Adjective embedding *(cold)*	Phrase

Rhyme Family

[-anks] *franks, (snow) banks, thanks*

Teaching Ideas

Introductory Sharing:	the two meanings of "hot dog"
Vocabulary Targets:	*hot dogs, cold, snow banks, chili, franks, bark*
Extension Activity:	Make a chili dog; cut it into pieces so all the children can have a taste.

Comments, Observations, and Additional Teaching Ideas

Hot dogs play in snow banks.   _____

The snow banks are cold.   in _____ snow banks.

They like chili.   _____

The chili is on their franks.   on _____.

They get these.   _____,

They bark, "Thanks!"   and _____!

Hot dogs play in snow banks.   Oh, _____

The snow banks are cold.   _____!

Chant 33: Irv's Curve   Level = E

Chant Model

Irv can pitch with speed and nerve.

He can throw a swooping curve.

He can make it loop and swerve.

Oh, Irv can pitch with speed and nerve!

Syntax Goals

Line 1	Noun coordination *(and)*	Phrase
Line 2	Participle embedding *(swooping)*	Phrase
Line 3	Verb coordination *(and)*	Phrase
Line 4	Noun coordination *(and)*	Phrase

Rhyme Families

[-erve] *curve, nerve, swerve*

[-oop] *loop, swoop(ing)*

[-ow] *oh, throw*

Teaching Ideas

Introductory Sharing: baseball; how to pitch a ball

Vocabulary Targets: *pitch, speed, nerve, throw, swooping, curve, loop, swerve*

Extension Activity: Have the children role-play pitching a ball to each other.

Comments, Observations, and Additional Teaching Ideas

Irv can pitch with speed.   _____

Irv can pitch with nerve.   _____ and _____.

He can throw a curve.   _____

The curve is swooping.   a _____ curve.

He can make it loop.   _____

He can make it swerve.   _____ and _____.

Irv can pitch with speed.   Oh, _____

Irv can pitch with nerve.   _____!

Chant 34: Jane's Sprain   Level = M

Chant Model

Jane ran swiftly in the lane.

Then she slipped and got a sprain.

On she zipped while feeling pain.

Oh, Jane ran swiftly in the lane!

Syntax Goals

Line 1	Preposition embedding *(in)*	Phrase
Line 2	Verb coordination *(and)*	Phrase
Line 3	Adverb embedding *(while)*	Phrase
Line 4	Preposition embedding *(in)*	Phrase

Rhyme Families

[-ain] *Jane, lane, pain, sprain*

[-ipt] *slipped, zipped*

Teaching Ideas

Introductory Sharing:	experiences with broken bones or sprained limbs; getting hurt when participating in a sport
Vocabulary Targets:	*swiftly, lane, slipped, sprain,* "*zipped,*" "*feeling pain*"
Extension Activity:	Bring in bandages. Have the children take turns wrapping each other's limbs and pretending to be hurt with a sprain.

Comments, Observations, and Additional Teaching Ideas

Jane ran swiftly. _____

She ran in the lane. in _____.

Then she slipped. _____

She got a sprain. and _____.

On she zipped. _____

She was feeling pain. while _____.

Jane ran swiftly. Oh, _____

She ran in the lane. _____!

Chant 35: Jerry's Goof   Level = M

Chant Model

Jerry made a giant goof.

He tried flying off our roof.

Sign his cast if you want proof.

Oh, Jerry made a giant goof!

Syntax Goals

Line 1	Adjective embedding *(giant)*	Phrase
Line 2	Preposition embedding *(off)*	Phrase
Line 3	Subordination (adverbial—*if*)	Clause
Line 4	Adjective embedding *(giant)*	Phrase

Rhyme Family

[-oof] *goof, proof, roof*

Teaching Ideas

Introductory Sharing:	experiences with broken bones or casts
Vocabulary Targets:	*giant, goof, "flying off," roof, sign, cast, proof*
Extension Activity:	Have each child wrap his or her arm with white paper to simulate a cast. Allow the children to sign each other's casts.

Comments, Observations, and Additional Teaching Ideas

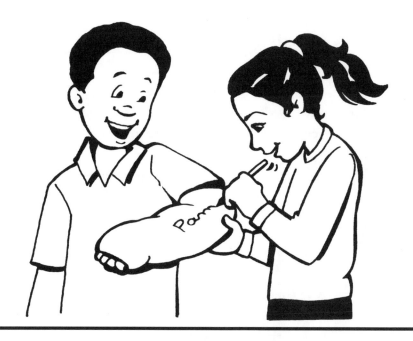

Jerry made a goof.   _____

The goof was giant.   a _____ goof.

He tried flying.   _____

He went off our roof.   off _____.

Sign his cast.   _____

You want proof.   if _____.

Jerry made a goof.   Oh, _____

The goof was giant.   _____!

Chant 36: Joel's Goal   Level = M

Chant Model

Joel is someone with a goal.

His main aim is rock and roll.

He'll play blues and then add soul.

Oh, Joel is someone with a goal!

Syntax Goals

Line 1	Preposition embedding *(with)*	Phrase
Line 2	Noun coordination *(and)*	Phrase
Line 3	Verb coordination *(and)*	Phrase
Line 4	Preposition embedding *(with)*	Phrase

Rhyme Family

[-ole] *goal, Joel, roll, soul*

Teaching Ideas

Introductory Sharing: types of music that the children like; playing a musical instrument

Vocabulary Targets: *goal, "main aim," "rock and roll," blues, add, soul*

Extension Activity: Play short segments of rock and roll, blues, and soul music to the group. Discuss the differences between the three types of music. Allow the children to vote for their favorite type. Chart and discuss the results of the voting.

Comments, Observations, and Additional Teaching Ideas

Joel is someone.   _____

He has a goal.   with _____.

His main aim is rock.   _____

His main aim is roll.   _____ and _____.

He'll play blues.   _____

He'll then add soul.   and _____.

Joel is someone.   Oh, _____

He has a goal.   _____!

Chant 37: Jogging Dogs   Level = D

Chant Model

While some dogs sleep, our
   sheepdogs jog.
They like to slog through creeping fog.
Watch them leap that rotten log.
Oh, while some dogs sleep, our
   sheepdogs jog!

Syntax Goals

Line 1	Subordination (adverbial—*while*)	Clause
Line 2	Participle embedding *(creeping)*	Phrase
Line 3	Adjective embedding *(rotten)*	Phrase
Line 4	Subordination (adverbial—*while*)	Clause

Rhyme Families

[-eep] *creep(ing), leap, sheep(dogs), sleep*
[-ew] *through, to*
[-og] *dog(s), fog, jog, log, sheepdog(s), slog*

Teaching Ideas

Introductory Sharing:	exercising pets; how dogs like to exercise; where you might find dogs running
Vocabulary Targets:	*sheepdogs, jog, slog, creeping, fog, leap, rotten, log*
Extension Activity:	Have the children cut pictures of running dogs out of magazines. Have each child tell or write a story about one picture.

Comments, Observations, and Additional Teaching Ideas

Some dogs sleep.   While _____,

But our sheepdogs jog.   _____.

They like to slog through fog.   _____

The fog is creeping.   through _____ fog.

Watch them leap that log.   _____

The log is rotten.   that _____ log.

Some dogs sleep.   Oh, _____,

But our sheepdogs jog.   _____!

Chant 38: Jungle Jim   Level = M

Chant Model

My friend's name is Jungle Jim.
Watch him swing beneath a limb.
Hear the sound that comes from him.
Oh, my friend's name is Jungle Jim!

Syntax Goals

Line 1	Possessive embedding *(friend's)*	Phrase
Line 2	Preposition embedding *(beneath)*	Phrase
Line 3	Subordination (relative—*that*)	Clause
Line 4	Possessive embedding *(friend's)*	Phrase

Rhyme Family

[-im] *him, Jim, limb*

Teaching Ideas

Introductory Sharing: how monkeys swing from limb to limb; types of trees that grow in the jungle; swinging from a rope

Vocabulary Targets: *jungle, swing, limb, sound, beneath*

Extension Activity: Take the children outside and have each child practice swinging on a rope swing or on the monkey bars.

Comments, Observations, and Additional Teaching Ideas

My friend has a name.   My friend's _____

It is Jungle Jim.   _____.

Watch him swing.   Watch _____

He swings beneath a limb.   _____.

Hear the sound.   _____

It comes from him.   that _____.

My friend has a name.   Oh, _____

It is Jungle Jim.   _____!

Chant 39: Kate Skates   Level = M

Chant Model

Kate skates early, then skates late.

She won't brag, but she skates great.

She skates curves, and she
skates straight.

Oh, Kate skates early, then skates late!

Syntax Goals

Line 1	Verb coordination *(then)*		Phrase
Line 2	Coordination *(but)*		Clause
Line 3	Coordination *(and)*		Clause
Line 4	Verb coordination *(then)*		Phrase

Rhyme Family

[-ate] *Kate, great, late, skate(s), straight*

Teaching Ideas

Introductory Sharing: Rollerblading and ice-skating experiences

Vocabulary Targets: *skates, early, late, brag, great, curves, straight*

Extension Activity: Bring in roller skates, ice skates, and Rollerblades. Discuss and write about the differences among the three types of skates.

Comments, Observations, and Additional Teaching Ideas

Kate skates early.   _____,

She skates late.   then _____.

She won't brag.   _____,

She skates great.   but _____.

She skates curves.   _____,

She skates straight.   and _____.

Kate skates early.   Oh, _____

She skates late.   _____!

Chant 40: Kate the Cat   Level = D

Chant Model

Kate is a cat that you love to hate.

She yowls and howls
when the hour is late.

She's loud and proud and overweight.

Oh, Kate is a cat that you love to hate!

Syntax Goals

Line 1	Subordination (relative—*that*)	Clause
Line 2	Subordination (adverbial—*when*)	Clause
Line 3	Adjective coordination *(and)*	Phrase
Line 4	Subordination (relative—*that*)	Clause

Rhyme Families

[-ate] *hate, Kate, late, overweight*

[-oud] *loud, proud*

[-owls] *howls, yowls*

Teaching Ideas

Introductory Sharing: cats as pets; yowling cats at night; pets who live outdoors; things pets do at night

Vocabulary Targets: *love, hate, yowl, howl, "late hour," loud, proud, "overweight"*

Extension Activity: Read the book *Have You Seen My Cat?* (1987) by Eric Carle, Natick, MA: Picture Book Studio.

Comments, Observations, and Additional Teaching Ideas

Kate is a cat. _____

You love to hate her.   that _____.

She yowls and howls.   _____

The hour is late.   when _____.

She's loud and proud.   _____

She's overweight.   and _____.

Kate is a cat.   Oh, _____

You love to hate her.   _____!

Chant 41: Kate's Lunch   Level = M

Chant Model

Watch Kate eat from off my plate.

She thinks that my lunch is great.

Kate may have a date with fate.

Oh, watch Kate eat from off my plate!

Syntax Goals

Line 1	Preposition embedding *(from off)*	Phrase
Line 2	Subordination (nominal—*that*)	Clause
Line 3	Preposition embedding *(with)*	Phrase
Line 4	Preposition embedding *(from off)*	Phrase

Rhyme Family

[-ate] *date, fate, great, Kate, plate*

Teaching Ideas

Introductory Sharing:	"people food" versus pet food; training pets not to eat off the table
Vocabulary Targets:	*watch, plate, think, lunch, great, "date with fate"*
Extension Activity:	Brainstorm "people food" that cats might like to eat. Write the names and/or draw pictures of the food items where all children can see.

Comments, Observations, and Additional Teaching Ideas

Watch Kate eat.   _____

She eats from off my plate.   from _____ .

She thinks something.   _____

My lunch is great.   that _____ .

Kate may have a date.   _____

Her date would be with fate.   with _____ .

Watch Kate eat.   Oh, _____

She eats from off my plate.   _____ !

Chant 42: Kick the Can   Level = M

Chant Model

Find a buddy if you can.

Then take aim, and kick the can.

You will be a kicking fan.

Oh, find a buddy if you can!

Syntax Goals

Line 1	Subordination (adverbial—*if*)	Clause
Line 2	Coordination *(and)*	Clause
Line 3	Participle embedding *(kicking)*	Phrase
Line 4	Subordination (adverbial—*if*)	Clause

Rhyme Family

[-an] *can, fan*

Teaching Ideas

Introductory Sharing: playing the game "Kick the Can"

Vocabulary Targets: *buddy,* "take aim," *kick, can* (noun and verb), *fan*

Extension Activity: Ask children to list their favorite outdoor games, including ones they have made up on their own.

Comments, Observations, and Additional Teaching Ideas

Find a buddy.   _____

You can.   if _____ .

Then take aim.   _____ ,

Kick the can.   and _____ .

You will be a fan.   _____

The fan is kicking.   a _____ fan.

Find a buddy.   Oh, _____

You can.   _____ !

Chant 43: Lime Slime   Level = M

Chant Model

You'll like slime when mixed with lime.

Slime is good most anytime.

Try a drink that is sublime.

Oh, you'll like slime when mixed
    with lime!

Syntax Goals

Line 1	Subordination (adverbial—*when*)	Clause
Line 2	Adverb embedding *(most anytime)*	Phrase
Line 3	Subordination (relative—*that*)	Clause
Line 4	Subordination (adverbial—*when*)	Clause

Rhyme Family

[-ime] *anytime, lime, slime, sublime*

Teaching Ideas

Introductory Sharing: experiences with unusual beverages or foods

Vocabulary Targets: *slime, mixed, lime, anytime, drink, sublime*

Extension Activity: Make a slime that the children can drink. Create an edible concoction using partially chilled Jello and soda pop or juice. Allow each child to sample the "slime."

Comments, Observations, and Additional Teaching Ideas

You'll like slime.   _____

Slime is mixed with lime.   when _____.

Slime is good.   _____

This is most anytime.   most _____.

Try a drink.   _____

The drink is sublime.   that _____.

You'll like slime.   Oh, _____

Slime is mixed with lime.   _____!

Chant 44: Lucille Seal   Level = M

Chant Model

Seals like Lucille just love to squeal.

She squeals out to get a meal.

Trout is a treat, or she'll eat eel.

Oh, seals like Lucille just love
to squeal!

Syntax Goals

Line 1	Preposition embedding *(like)*	Phrase
Line 2	Infinitive embedding *([in order] to)*	Phrase
Line 3	Coordination *(or)*	Clause
Line 4	Preposition embedding *(like)*	Phrase

Rhyme Families

[-eal] *eel, Lucille, meal, seal(s), she'll, squeal*

[-eat] *eat, treat*

[-out] *out, trout*

Teaching Ideas

Introductory Sharing: seeing seals make noise and do tricks at a zoo or park

Vocabulary Targets: seal, squeal, meal, trout, treat, eel

Extension Activity: Read the book *Seal Pup Grows Up! The Story of a Harbor Seal* (1994)
by Kathleen Weidner Zoehfeld, New York: Scholastic.

Comments, Observations, and Additional Teaching Ideas

Seals just love to squeal.

Seals like _____

They are like Lucille.

_____.

She squeals out.

_____

This is to get a meal.

to _____.

Trout is a treat.

_____,

She'll eat eel.

or _____.

Seals just love to squeal.

Oh, _____

They are like Lucille.

_____!

Chant 45: Lunch Bunch   Level = D

Chant Model

Our class is a hungry bunch.

When noon arrives, we all want lunch.

Some kids munch, while others crunch.

Oh, our class is a hungry bunch!

Syntax Goals

Line 1	Adjective embedding *(hungry)*	Phrase
Line 2	Subordination (adverbial—*when*)	Clause
Line 3	Subordination (adverbial—*while*)	Clause
Line 4	Adjective embedding *(hungry)*	Phrase

Rhyme Family

[-unch] *bunch, crunch, lunch, munch*

Teaching Ideas

Introductory Sharing: what students like to eat for lunch; favorite foods; feeling very hungry right before lunchtime

Vocabulary Targets: *class, hungry, bunch, noon, arrives, lunch, munch, crunch*

Extension Activity: Discuss foods people eat for lunch versus those foods eaten at breakfast, supper, or snack time. List the foods mentioned where all students can see them. Use a semantic web or map to group the foods that are named.

Comments, Observations, and Additional Teaching Ideas

Our class is a bunch.   _____

The bunch is hungry.   a _____bunch.

Noon arrives.   When _____,

We all want lunch.   _____.

Some kids munch.   _____,

Others crunch.   while _____.

Our class is a bunch.   Oh, _____

The bunch is hungry.   _____!

131

Chant 46: Math Gal　　　　　　　　　　　　　　　　Level = D

Chant Model

Gail is a gal who likes her math.
Gail counts rocks along the path.
She clocks time while in the bath.
Oh, Gail is a gal who likes her math!

Syntax Goals

Line 1	Subordination (relative—*who*)	Clause
Line 2	Preposition embedding *(along)*	Phrase
Line 3	Adverb embedding *(while)*	Phrase
Line 4	Subordination (relative—*who*)	Clause

Rhyme Families

[-ath] *bath, math, path*
[-ocks] *clocks, rocks*

Teaching Ideas

Introductory Sharing:　ways we use numbers throughout the day

Vocabulary Targets:　*gal, math, counts, rocks, along, path, "clocks time," bath*

Extension Activity:　Assign each child to count something in the room (e.g., pieces of chalk on the ledge, chairs, tiles on the ceiling, books on the shelf). Have each child report his or her findings back to the group.

Comments, Observations, and Additional Teaching Ideas

Gail is a gal.   _____

She likes her math.   who _____.

Gail counts rocks.   _____

They are along the path.   along _____.

She clocks time.   _____

She is in the bath.   while _____.

Gail is a gal.   Oh, _____

She likes her math.   _____!

Chant 47: Milk Shake Cow   Level = D

Chant Model

Milk is a drink that our cow makes.

She makes milk with no mistakes.

When she jumps, we have milk shakes.

Oh, milk is a drink that our cow makes!

Syntax Goals

Line 1	Subordination (relative—*that*)	Clause
Line 2	Preposition embedding *(with)*	Phrase
Line 3	Subordination (adverbial—*when*)	Clause
Line 4	Subordination (relative—*that*)	Clause

Rhyme Families

[-akes] *makes, mistakes, (milk) shakes*

[-ee] *she, we*

[-ow] *no, oh*

Teaching Ideas

Introductory Sharing:	milking cows; how to make milk shakes
Vocabulary Targets:	*drink, cow, "makes milk," mistakes, jumps, milk shakes*
Extension Activity:	Bring in the ingredients to make milk shakes with the children. Invite the children to sample the milk shakes.

Comments, Observations, and Additional Teaching Ideas

Milk is a drink.

_____

Our cow makes it.

that _____.

She makes milk.

_____

She makes no mistakes.

with _____.

She jumps.

When _____,

We have milk shakes.

we _____.

Milk is a drink.

Oh, _____

Our cow makes it.

_____!

Chant 48: Mona the Mouse   Level = M

Chant Model

Mona is a mouse that you can't hear.

She roams the house when the
coast is clear.

She eats many treats without any fear.

Oh, Mona is a mouse that you
can't hear!

Syntax Goals

Line 1	Subordination (relative—*that*)	Clause
Line 2	Subordination (adverbial—*when*)	Clause
Line 3	Preposition embedding *(without)*	Phrase
Line 4	Subordination (relative—*that*)	Clause

Rhyme Families

[-eats] *eats, treats*

[-eer] *clear, fear, hear*

[-ouse] *house, mouse*

Teaching Ideas

Introductory Sharing: what mice eat; catching mice; where mice hide

Vocabulary Targets: *mouse, hear, roams, "coast is clear," treats, fear*

Extension Activity: Read the book *Town Mouse and Country Mouse* (1987) by Janet
Stevens, New York: Holiday House. Or read a different version of the
city mouse/country mouse story.

Comments, Observations, and Additional Teaching Ideas

Mona is a mouse.

You can't hear her.   that _____.

She roams the house.

The coast is clear.   when _____.

She eats many treats.

She is without any fear.   without _____.

Mona is a mouse.   Oh, _____

You can't hear her.   _____!

Chant 49: My Friend Paul   Level = D

Chant Model

I have a friend whose name is Paul.

He has a bat, and I have a ball.

Pitches he hits go over the wall.

Oh, I have a friend whose name is Paul!

Syntax Goals

Line 1	Subordination (relative—*whose*)	Clause
Line 2	Coordination *(and)*	Clause
Line 3	Subordination (relative—*[that]*)	Clause
Line 4	Subordination (relative—*whose*)	Clause

Rhyme Families

[-awl] *ball, Paul, wall*

[-ow] *go, oh*

Teaching Ideas

Introductory Sharing: playing sports with friends; favorite team sports; playing baseball

Vocabulary Targets: *pitches, hits, "over the wall"*

Extension Activity: Have the children make lists of their closest friends' names. Next to each friend's name, tell the children to write the name of the sport or activity they like to play with that friend.

Comments, Observations, and Additional Teaching Ideas

I have a friend.

_____

His name is Paul.

whose _____.

He has a bat.

_____,

I have a ball.

and _____.

Pitches go over the wall.

Pitches _____

He hits pitches.

go _____.

I have a friend.

Oh, _____

His name is Paul.

_____!

Chant 50: Nachos   Level = M

Chant Model

We like nachos with melted cheese.	
We pig out on snacks like these.	
We say nachos are sure to please.	
Oh, we like nachos with melted cheese!	

Syntax Goals

Line 1	Preposition embedding *(with)*	Phrase
Line 2	Preposition embedding *(like)*	Phrase
Line 3	Subordination (nominal—*[that]*)	Clause
Line 4	Preposition embedding *(with)*	Phrase

Rhyme Family

[-ease] *cheese, please, these*

Teaching Ideas

Introductory Sharing:	making and/or eating nachos
Vocabulary Targets:	nachos, melted cheese, "pig out," snacks, "sure to please"
Extension Activity:	Bring in tortilla chips and cheese sauce. Prepare and eat nachos with the students.

Comments, Observations, and Additional Teaching Ideas

We like nachos.   _____

They have melted cheese.   with _____.

We pig out on snacks.   We _____

The snacks are like these.   _____.

We say something.   _____ nachos

Nachos are sure to please.   _____ please.

We like nachos.   Oh, _____

They have melted cheese.   _____!

Chant 51: Nate the Skater   Level = M

Chant Model

Nate likes skating on the ice.
Slide and glide feel oh-so-nice!
He makes "eights" by circling twice.
Oh, Nate likes skating on the ice!

Syntax Goals

Line 1	Preposition embedding *(on)*	Phrase
Line 2	Noun coordination *(and + feel)*	Phrase
Line 3	Preposition embedding *(by)*	Phrase
Line 4	Preposition embedding *(on)*	Phrase

Rhyme Families

[-ate] *eight(s), Nate, skat(ing)*
[-ice] *ice, nice, twice*
[-ide] *glide, slide*
[-ow] *oh, so*

Teaching Ideas

Introductory Sharing: ice-skating; where to ice-skate; equipment needed to ice-skate
Vocabulary Targets: *skating, slide, glide, "eights," circling, twice, "feels oh-so-nice"*
Extension Activity: Have the students make "figure eights" by circling their finger twice on various surfaces (e.g., dusty chalkboard, sandy sidewalk, foggy window).

Comments, Observations, and Additional Teaching Ideas

Nate likes skating.   _____

He skates on the ice.   on _____.

Slide feels oh-so-nice!   _____ and _____

Glide feels oh-so-nice!   _____!

He makes "eights."   _____

This is by circling twice.   by _____.

Nate likes skating.   Oh, _____

He skates on the ice.   _____!

Chant 52: Nice Ice   Level = D

Chant Model

School closed twice because of ice.
Our days off were cold but nice.
When June comes, we'll pay the price.
Oh, school closed twice because of ice!

Syntax Goals

Line 1	Preposition embedding *(because of)*	Phrase
Line 2	Adjective coordination *(but)*	Phrase
Line 3	Subordination (adverbial—*when*)	Clause
Line 4	Preposition embedding *(because of)*	Phrase

Rhyme Families

[-ay] *day(s), pay*
[-ice] *ice, nice, price, twice*

Teaching Ideas

Introductory Sharing:	weather conditions that can cause schools to close temporarily; what happens when school is canceled for the day; making up missed time and work
Vocabulary Targets:	*"school closed," twice, ice, "days off," June, "pay the price"*
Extension Activity:	Discuss what parents and students should do to find out if school is closed due to weather conditions. Make a list of several activities that students like to do when school is closed for the day. Tally how many students enjoy each activity. Compare activities to determine which are most popular.

Comments, Observations, and Additional Teaching Ideas

School closed twice.   _____

This was because of ice.   because _____.

Our days off were cold.   _____

Our days off were nice.   _____ but _____.

June comes.   When _____,

We'll pay the price.   _____.

School closed twice.   Oh, _____

This was because of ice.   _____!

Chant 53: Numb Thumb   Level = E

Chant Model

I did something that was dumb.

I swung hard and hit my thumb.

Now it's red and turning numb.

Oh, I did something that was dumb!

Syntax Goals

Line 1	Subordination (relative—*that*)	Clause
Line 2	Verb coordination *(and)*	Phrase
Line 3	Adjective coordination *(and)*	Phrase
Line 4	Subordination (relative—*that*)	Clause

Rhyme Families

[-it] *hit, it('s)*

[-um] *dumb, numb, thumb*

[-y] *I, my*

Teaching Ideas

Introductory Sharing:	what it feels like to accidentally hit your thumb with a hammer; what it feels like when a body part is numb
Vocabulary Targets:	*dumb, swung, hard, hit, thumb, red, "turning numb"*
Extension Activity:	Practice pounding large nails into styrofoam, cardboard tubes, or tagboard using soft mallets or toy hammers. Discuss the need to work carefully and precisely when hammering.

Comments, Observations, and Additional Teaching Ideas

I did something.   _____

It was dumb.   that _____.

I swung hard.   _____

I hit my thumb.   and _____.

Now it's red.   _____

Now it's turning numb.   and _____.

I did something.   Oh, _____

It was dumb.   _____!

Chant 54: Park Shark   Level = E

Chant Model

We went splashing at the park.
How we thrashed till after dark.
Then we saw a scary shark.
Oh, we went splashing at the park!

Syntax Goals

Line 1	Preposition embedding *(at)*	Phrase
Line 2	Preposition embedding *(till)*	Phrase
Line 3	Adjective embedding *(scary)*	Phrase
Line 4	Preposition embedding *(at)*	Phrase

Rhyme Families

[-ark] *dark, park, shark*
[-ash] *splash(ing), thrash(ed)*

Teaching Ideas

Introductory Sharing: beach parks; swimming in the ocean; sharks

Vocabulary Targets: *splashing, park, thrashed, after, dark, scary, shark*

Extension Activity: Bring in a toy shark to look at while brainstorming shark facts. Write the facts where all students can see them using a semantic web to group the ideas (e.g., where sharks are found, what they eat, how they look, what they do).

Comments, Observations, and Additional Teaching Ideas

We went splashing.   _____

This was at the park.   at _____.

How we thrashed.   _____

It was till after dark.   till _____.

Then we saw a shark.   _____

The shark was scary.   a _____ shark.

We went splashing.   Oh, _____

This was at the park.   _____!

Chant 55: Pat's Cats   Level = E

Chant Model

Pat likes cats, and they like her.

She pets them, and how they purr.

Their sounds are soft just like their fur.

Oh, Pat likes cats, and they like her!

Syntax Goals

Line 1	Coordination *(and)*	Clause
Line 2	Coordination *(and)*	Clause
Line 3	Preposition embedding *(like)*	Phrase
Line 4	Coordination *(and)*	Clause

Rhyme Families

[-at] *cat(s), Pat*

[-er] *fur, her, purr*

Teaching Ideas

Introductory Sharing: cats as pets; characteristics of cats

Vocabulary Targets: *pet, purr, "sounds are soft," fur*

Extension Activity: Bring in a cat in a pet carrier; let the children pet it and listen to it purr.

Comments, Observations, and Additional Teaching Ideas

Pat likes cats.   _____,

They like her.   and _____.

She pets them.   _____,

How they purr.   and _____.

Their sounds are soft.   _____

This is just like their fur.   just _____.

Pat likes cats.   Oh, _____,

They like her!   _____!

151

Chant 56: Pesky Guest
Level = M

Chant Model

Our guest bragged that he was best.

He claimed fame from east to west.

Pests like him don't seem to rest.

Oh, our guest bragged that he was best!

Syntax Goals

Line 1	Subordination (nominal—*that*)	Clause
Line 2	Preposition embedding *(from)*	Phrase
Line 3	Preposition embedding *(like)*	Phrase
Line 4	Subordination (nominal—*that*)	Clause

Rhyme Families

[-ame] *claim(ed), fame*

[-est] *best, guest, pest(s), rest, west*

Teaching Ideas

Introductory Sharing:	examples of bragging; how it makes you feel when a classmate brags
Vocabulary Targets:	*pesky, guest, bragged, best,* "claimed fame," "east to west," *pest, rest*
Extension Activity:	Read the book *Mufaro's Beautiful Daughters: An African Tale* (1987) by J. Steptoe, New York: Lothrop, Lee, and Shepard.

Comments, Observations, and Additional Teaching Ideas

Our guest bragged something. _____

He was best.   that _____.

He claimed fame.   _____

It was from east to west.   from _____.

Pests don't seem to rest.   Pests like _____

Pests are like him.   _____.

Our guest bragged something.   Oh, _____

He was best.   _____!

Chant 57: Pet Hen   Level = M

Chant Model

Glen and Gwen have raised a hen.

She's a pet that has no pen.

Her cute chicks now number 10.

Oh, Glen and Gwen have raised a hen!

Syntax Goals

Line 1	Noun coordination *(and + have)*	Phrase
Line 2	Subordination *(relative—that)*	Clause
Line 3	Adjective embedding *(cute)*	Phrase
Line 4	Noun coordination *(and + have)*	Phrase

Rhyme Families

[-en] *Glen, Gwen, hen, pen, ten*

[-ow] *no, oh*

Teaching Ideas

Introductory Sharing:	hens; chickens; eggs; pets on a farm
Vocabulary Targets:	*raised, hen, pet, pen, cute, chicks, "number 10"*
Extension Activity:	Bring in baby chicks or pictures of chicks. Discuss how to care for baby chicks.

Comments, Observations, and Additional Teaching Ideas

Glen has raised a hen. _____

Gwen has raised a hen. have _____.

She's a pet. _____

The pet has no pen. that _____.

Her chicks now number 10. Her _____ chicks

Her chicks are cute. _____.

Glen has raised a hen. Oh, _____

Gwen has raised a hen. _____!

155

Chant 58: Pet Pig   Level = D

Chant Model

Out in the pen is my pet pig.
Where there's mud, she loves to dig.
She once was small, but now she's big.
Oh, out in the pen is my pet pig!

Syntax Goals

Line 1	Noun embedding *(pet)*	Phrase
Line 2	Subordination (adverbial—*where*)	Clause
Line 3	Coordination *(but)*	Clause
Line 4	Noun embedding *(pet)*	Phrase

Rhyme Families

[-are] *there('s), where*
[-ig] *big, dig, pig*

Teaching Ideas

Introductory Sharing: experiences with farms, pigs, or mud

Vocabulary Targets: *pen, pet, pig, mud, loves, dig, once, small, now, big*

Extension Activity: Show pictures of a baby pig and a grown pig; compare the differences between the two different pigs. Talk about how people raise potbelly pigs as pets, and show pictures if available.

Comments, Observations, and Additional Teaching Ideas

Out in the pen is my pig.   _____

The pig is my pet.   my _____ pig.

There's mud.   Where _____,

She loves to dig.   _____.

She once was small.   _____,

Now she's big.   but _____.

Out in the pen is my pig.   Oh, _____

The pig is my pet.   _____!

Chant 59: Popcorn   Level = E

Chant Mode

Popcorn is my favorite food.

Its crunch gives me a friendly mood.

Munching is not rude or crude.

Oh, popcorn is my favorite food!

Syntax Goals

Line 1	Adjective embedding *(favorite)*	Phrase
Line 2	Adjective embedding *(friendly)*	Phrase
Line 3	Adjective coordination *(or)*	Phrase
Line 4	Adjective embedding *(favorite)*	Phrase

Rhyme Families

[-ude] *crude, food, mood, rude*

[-unch] *crunch, munch(ing)*

Teaching Ideas

Introductory Sharing: favorite times or places for eating popcorn; favorite foods

Vocabulary Targets: *popcorn, favorite, food, crunch, "friendly mood," munching, rude, crude*

Extension Activity: Make popcorn together and share it. Talk about what creates a friendly mood.

Comments, Observations, and Additional Teaching Ideas

Popcorn is a food.   _____

It is my favorite.   my _____ food.

Its crunch gives me a mood.   _____

The mood is friendly.   a _____ mood.

Munching is not rude.   _____

Munching is not crude.   _____ or _____.

Popcorn is a food.   Oh, _____

It is my favorite.   _____!

Chant 60: Portland Fog   Level = E

Chant Model

Portland has its rain and fog.

Folks wear waders when they jog.

Each kid has a slug or frog.

Oh, Portland has its rain and fog!

Syntax Goals

Line 1	Noun coordination *(and)*	Phrase
Line 2	Subordination (adverbial—*when*)	Clause
Line 3	Noun coordination *(or)*	Phrase
Line 4	Noun coordination *(and)*	Phrase

Rhyme Family

[-og] *fog, frog, jog*

Teaching Ideas

Introductory Sharing:	slugs and frogs as pets; what to wear in the rain and fog
Vocabulary Targets:	*Portland, rain, fog, folks, waders, jog, slug, frog*
Extension Activity:	Bring a slug or frog to class, and have the children observe and discuss its actions. Talk about why Portland is a good place for a slug or frog to live.

Comments, Observations, and Additional Teaching Ideas

Portland has its rain.   _____

Portland has its fog.   _____ and _____.

Folks wear waders.   _____

They jog.   when _____.

Each kid has a slug.   _____

Each kid has a frog.   _____ or _____.

Portland has its rain.   Oh, _____

Portland has its fog.   _____!

Chant 61: Reading at Night   Level = D

Chant Model

Late at night, I like to read.

Soon words blur, which slows my speed.

Then I know it's sleep I need.

Oh, late at night, I like to read!

Syntax Goals

Line 1	Adverb embedding *(late at night)*	Phrase
Line 2	Subordination (relative—*which*)	Clause
Line 3	Subordination (nominal—*[that])*	Clause
Line 4	Adverb embedding *(late at night)*	Phrase

Rhyme Families

[-eed] *need, read, speed*

[-ow] *slow(s), know, oh*

[-y] *I, my*

Teaching Ideas

Introductory Sharing: bedtime stories; reading to fall asleep

Vocabulary Targets: *late, night, read, soon, "words blur," slow, speed, sleep, need*

Extension Activity: Discuss where some creatures sleep (e.g., a frog on a lily pad, a bird in a nest).

Comments, Observations, and Additional Teaching Ideas

I like to read.	Late _____,
It is late at night.	I _____.
Soon words blur.	_____,
This slows my speed.	which _____.
Then I know something.	_____
It's sleep I need.	it's _____.
I like to read.	Oh, _____,
It is late at night.	_____!

Chant 62: Red Ants   Level = E

Chant Model

Once I lost my pet red ants.

Then I found them in my pants.

Ants and I did quite a dance.

Oh, once I lost my pet red ants!

Syntax Goals

Line 1	Noun embedding *(pet)*	Phrase
Line 2	Preposition embedding *(in)*	Phrase
Line 3	Noun coordination *(and)*	Phrase
Line 4	Noun embedding *(pet)*	Phrase

Rhyme Families

[-ance] *ants, dance, pants*

[-y] *I, my*

Teaching Ideas

Introductory Sharing:	losing a pet; how it feels to get a bug in your clothing
Vocabulary Targets:	*lost, pet, red ants, found, pants, quite, dance*
Extension Activity:	Bring an ant farm to class; observe and discuss the ants' activities.

Comments, Observations, and Additional Teaching Ideas

Once I lost my red ants.   _____

The ants were pets.   my _____ ants.

Then I found them.   _____

They were in my pants.   in _____.

Ants did quite a dance.   _____ and _____

I did quite a dance.   _____.

Once I lost my red ants.   Oh, _____

The ants were pets.   _____!

Chant 63: Rhythm, Rhyme, and Rap   Level = D

Chant Model

We want rhythm, rhyme, and rap.

For our group, it's such a snap.

Our toes tap while our hands clap.

Oh, we want rhythm, rhyme, and rap!

Syntax Goals

Line 1	Noun coordination *(and)*	Phrase
Line 2	Preposition embedding *(for)*	Phrase
Line 3	Subordination (adverbial—*while)*	Clause
Line 4	Noun coordination *(and)*	Phrase

Rhyme Family

[-ap] *clap, rap, snap, tap*

Teaching Ideas

Introductory Sharing: favorite music; rap music

Vocabulary Targets: *rhythm, rhyme, rap, group, snap,* "toes tap," "hands clap"

Extension Activity: Listen to a brief recorded rap. Have the children snap their fingers or tap their toes to the rhythm.

Comments, Observations, and Additional Teaching Ideas

We want rhythm.   _____,

We want rhyme and rap.   _____, and _____.

It's such a snap.   For _____,

This is for our group.   _____.

Our toes tap.   _____

Our hands clap.   while _____.

We want rhythm.   Oh, _____,

We want rhyme and rap.   _____, and _____!

Chant 64: Rice Pudding   Level = E

Chant Model

We like pudding, and we like rice.

Put rice in our pudding, and it's
twice as nice.

Put mice in our pudding, and it's
not so nice.

Oh, we like pudding, and we like rice!

Syntax Goals

Line 1	Coordination *(and)*	Clause
Line 2	Coordination *(and)*	Clause
Line 3	Coordination *(and)*	Clause
Line 4	Coordination *(and)*	Clause

Rhyme Families

[-ice] *mice, nice, rice, twice*

[-ow] *oh, so*

Teaching Ideas

Introductory Sharing:	making or eating rice pudding; finding animals or bugs in food
Vocabulary Targets:	*pudding, rice, "twice as nice," mice, "not so nice"*
Extension Activity:	Bring pudding and rice pudding to class for the children to taste.

Comments, Observations, and Additional Teaching Ideas

We like pudding.   _____,

We like rice.   and _____.

Put rice in our pudding.   _____,

It's twice as nice.   and _____.

Put mice in our pudding.   _____,

It's not so nice.   and _____.

We like pudding.   Oh, _____,

We like rice.   _____!

Chant 65: River Raft   Level = D

Chant Model

While Taft worked, the
    neighbors laughed.
Taft took care and built his craft.
Now he floats a river raft.
Oh, while Taft worked, the
    neighbors laughed!

Syntax Goals

Line 1	Subordination (adverbial—*while*)	Clause
Line 2	Verb coordination *(and)*	Phrase
Line 3	Noun embedding *(river)*	Phrase
Line 4	Subordination (adverbial—*while*)	Clause

Rhyme Family

[-aft] *craft, laughed, raft, Taft*

Teaching Ideas

Introductory Sharing:	boat or rafting experiences
Vocabulary Targets:	*neighbor, laugh, "take care," built, craft, float, "river raft"*
Extension Activity:	Bring in a toy raft and let the children float it in a tub of water.

Comments, Observations, and Additional Teaching Ideas

Taft worked.

While _____,

The neighbors laughed.

_____.

Taft took care.

_____

He built his craft.

and _____.

Now he floats a raft.

_____

It is for the river.

a _____ raft.

Taft worked.

Oh, _____,

The neighbors laughed.

_____.

Chant 66: Rob the Robot   Level = D

Chant Model

Rob the robot knows a lot.

He remembers what he's taught.

On quiz shows he's really hot.

Oh, Rob the robot knows a lot!

Syntax Goals

Line 1	Appositive noun embedding *(the robot)*	Phrase
Line 2	Subordination (nominal—*what*)	Clause
Line 3	Preposition embedding *(on)*	Phrase
Line 4	Appositive noun embedding *(the robot)*	Phrase

Rhyme Families

[-ose] *knows, shows*

[-ot] *hot, lot, robot, taught*

Teaching Ideas

Introductory Sharing:	robots; favorite quiz shows; trivia games
Vocabulary Targets:	*robot, "knows a lot," remembers, taught, quiz shows, "really hot"*
Extension Activity:	Play a children's trivia game with the students.

Comments, Observations, and Additional Teaching Ideas

Rob knows a lot. _____

He is a robot. knows _____.

He remembers something. _____

It is what he's taught. what _____.

He's really hot. On _____

He's on quiz shows. _____.

Rob knows a lot. Oh, _____

He is a robot. _____!

Chant 67: Rock Climbing   Level = D

Chant Model

We groped slowly up the slope.

Working hard, we gripped the rope.

As we climbed, we kept up hope.

Oh, we groped slowly up the slope!

Syntax Goals

Line 1	Adverb embedding	(slowly)	Phrase
Line 2	Participle embedding	(working)	Phrase
Line 3	Subordination (adverbial—as)		Clause
Line 4	Adverb embedding	(slowly)	Phrase

Rhyme Family

[-ope] *grope(d), hope, rope, slope*

Teaching Ideas

Introductory Sharing:	rock climbing experiences
Vocabulary Targets:	*rock climbing, groped, slowly, slope, "working hard," gripped, rope, "keep hope"*
Extension Activity:	Show a picture of a rock climber. Using a rope, demonstrate gripping and pulling.

Comments, Observations, and Additional Teaching Ideas

We groped up the slope. _____

We groped slowly. up _____.

We were working hard. Working _____,

We gripped the rope. _____.

We climbed. As _____,

We kept up hope. _____.

We groped up the slope. Oh, _____

We groped slowly. _____!

Chant 68: Rollerblade Wade   Level = M

Chant Model

		Syntax Goals	
Wade got blades and pads on trade.	Line 1	Noun coordination (and)	Phrase
He says that he's got it made.	Line 2	Subordination (nominal—that)	Clause
Watch him scoot through sun and shade.	Line 3	Noun coordination (and)	Phrase
Oh, Wade got blades and pads on trade!	Line 4	Noun coordination (and)	Phrase

Rhyme Family

[-ade] *blade(s), made, shade, trade, Wade*

Teaching Ideas

Introductory Sharing:	experiences with Rollerblades
Vocabulary Targets:	*Rollerblade, pads, "on trade," "got it made," scoot, sun, shade*
Extension Activity:	Bring in a pair of Rollerblades and protective equipment for Rollerblading (e.g., helmet, knee pads, wrist guards). Discuss the importance of wearing the protective gear.

Comments, Observations, and Additional Teaching Ideas

Wade got blades on trade.   _____

Wade got pads on trade.   and _____.

He says something.   _____ that

He's got it made.   _____.

Watch him scoot through sun.   _____

Watch him scoot through shade.   _____ and _____.

Wade got blades on trade.   Oh, _____

Wade got pads on trade.   _____!

Chant 69: Rose's Clothes   Level = D

Chant Model

Rose is a lady who likes new clothes.

She shops stores until they close.

As she shops, her wardrobe grows.

Oh, Rose is a lady who likes
   new clothes!

Syntax Goals

Line 1	Subordination (relative—*who*)	Clause
Line 2	Subordination (adverbial—*until*)	Clause
Line 3	Subordination (adverbial—*as*)	Clause
Line 4	Subordination (relative—*who*)	Clause

Rhyme Families

[-ew] *new, who*

[-ose] *close, clothes, grows, Rose*

Teaching Ideas

Introductory Sharing:	experiences shopping for clothes at the mall
Vocabulary Targets:	*"new clothes," shop, stores, until, close, wardrobe, grows*
Extension Activity:	Have the children talk about new clothes they bought for school. List the clothing where all students can see them using a semantic web or map to group the ideas (e.g., tops, bottoms, footwear, accessories, outdoor clothing).

Comments, Observations, and Additional Teaching Ideas

Rose is a lady.

    _____

She likes new clothes.

    who _____.

She shops stores.

    _____

She shops until they close.

    until _____.

She shops.

    As _____,

Her wardrobe grows.

    _____.

Rose is a lady.

    Oh, _____

She likes new clothes.

    _____!

Chant 70: Rude Dude   Level = M

Chant Model

Jude is a dude who is quite rude.

First Jude burps, then slurps my food.

Worst of all is his bad mood.

Oh, Jude is a dude who is quite rude!

Syntax Goals

Line 1	Subordination (relative—*who*)	Clause
Line 2	Verb coordination *(then)*	Phrase
Line 3	Adjective embedding *(bad)*	Phrase
Line 4	Subordination (relative—*who*)	Clause

Rhyme Families

[-is] *his, is*

[-ude] *dude, food, Jude, mood, rude*

[-urps] *burps, slurps*

[-urst] *first, worst*

Teaching Ideas

Introductory Sharing: table manners; how people act when in bad moods

Vocabulary Targets: *dude, rude, first, burps, slurps, "worst of all," "bad mood"*

Extension Activity: Discuss proper and improper table manners. Write the ideas where everyone can see them under the headings "proper" and "improper." Have the students role-play proper table manners.

Comments, Observations, and Additional Teaching Ideas

Jude is a dude.   _____

He is quite rude.   who _____ .

First Jude burps.   _____ ,

He then slurps my food.   then _____ .

Worst of all is his mood.   _____

His mood is bad.   his _____ mood.

Jude is a dude.   Oh, _____

He is quite rude.   _____ !

Chant 71: Sad Chad   Level = D

Chant Model

Chad is a lad who is very sad.

His dad just found a book Chad had.

The book was bad, which made
   Dad mad.

Oh, Chad is a lad who is very sad!

Syntax Goals

Line 1	Subordination (relative—*who*)	Clause
Line 2	Subordination (relative—*[that]*)	Clause
Line 3	Subordination (relative—*which*)	Clause
Line 4	Subordination (relative—*who*)	Clause

Rhyme Families

[-ad] *bad, Chad, dad, had, lad, mad, sad*

[-is] *his, is*

Teaching Ideas

Introductory Sharing: books that children like to read; borrowing books from libraries

Vocabulary Targets: *lad, found, "make mad"*

Extension Activity: Take the children to the library. Check out a book to read aloud to the children. Encourage each child to check out a book.

Comments, Observations, and Additional Teaching Ideas

Chad is a lad.   _____

He is very sad.   who _____.

His dad just found a book. _____

Chad had it.   _____ had.

The book was bad.   _____,

This made Dad mad.   which _____.

Chad is a lad.   Oh, _____

He is very sad.   _____!

Chant 72: School Is Cool   Level = M

Chant Model

We like school because it's cool.

There we learn the golden rule.

Kids are nice and never cruel.

Oh, we like school because it's cool!

Syntax Goals

Line 1   Subordination (adverbial—*because*) Clause

Line 2   Adjective embedding *(golden)*   Phrase

Line 3   Adjective coordination *(and)*   Phrase

Line 4   Subordination (adverbial—*because*) Clause

Rhyme Family

[-ool] *cool, cruel, rule, school*

Teaching Ideas

Introductory Sharing: things we like about school; nice friends

Vocabulary Targets: *"cool," learn, "golden rule," never, cruel*

Extension Activity: Write the golden rule *("Do unto others as you want them to do unto you")* for all to see. Discuss the meaning of the saying.

Comments, Observations, and Additional Teaching Ideas

We like school.   _____

It's cool.   because _____.

There we learn the rule.   _____

The rule is golden.   the _____ rule.

Kids are nice.   _____

They are never cruel.   and _____.

We like school.   Oh, _____

It's cool.   _____!

Chant 73: Sharks   Level = D

Chant Model

Sharks can't bark, but they can bite.

They have teeth which are quite white.

If you see one, please take flight.

Oh, sharks can't bark, but they can bite!

Syntax Goals

Line 1	Coordination *(but)*		Clause
Line 2	Subordination (relative—*which*)		Clause
Line 3	Subordination (adverbial—*if*)		Clause
Line 4	Coordination *(but)*		Clause

Rhyme Families

[-ark] *bark, shark(s)*

[-ite] *bite, flight, quite, white*

Teaching Ideas

Introductory Sharing: animals that bark and/or bite; where you find sharks

Vocabulary Targets: *sharks, bark, bite, teeth, "quite white," "take flight"*

Extension Activity: Bring in a toy shark or show a picture of a shark displaying its teeth. Talk about where it would be common to see sharks and how to stay safe from sharks.

Comments, Observations, and Additional Teaching Ideas

Sharks can't bark.	_____,
They can bite.	but _____.
They have teeth.	_____
The teeth are quite white.	which _____.
You see one.	If _____,
Please take flight.	_____.
Sharks can't bark.	Oh, _____,
They can bite.	_____!

Chant 74: Shower Power   Level = D

Chant Model

Thad is a lad who loves our shower.

He opened the tap for half an hour.

He showered till noon, which used up power.

Oh, Thad is a lad who loves our shower!

Syntax Goals

Line 1	Subordination (relative—*who*)	Clause
Line 2	Preposition embedding *(for)*	Phrase
Line 3	Subordination (relative—*which*)	Clause
Line 4	Subordination (relative—*who*)	Clause

Rhyme Families

[-ad] *lad, Thad*

[-our] *hour, our, power, shower*

Teaching Ideas

Introductory Sharing: showering versus bathing; a rain shower versus a bathroom shower

Vocabulary Targets: *lad, shower,* "opened the tap," "half an hour," *noon,* "used up," *power*

Extension Activity: Discuss ways to save water at home—inside and outside. List the ideas where all students can see them, making groups under the headings "inside" and "outside."

Comments, Observations, and Additional Teaching Ideas

Thad is a lad.   _____

He loves our shower.   who _____.

He opened the tap.   _____

This was for half an hour.   for _____.

He showered till noon.   _____,

He used up power.   which _____.

Thad is a lad.   Oh, _____

He loves our shower.   _____!

Chant 75: Shrimp Feast   Level = D

Chant Model

Please don't skimp when you
  serve shrimp.
I'll feast on shrimp until I'm limp.
I'll become a shrimp-filled blimp.
Oh, please don't skimp when you
  serve shrimp!

Syntax Goals

Line 1	Subordination (adverbial—*when*)	Clause
Line 2	Subordination (adverbial—*until*)	Clause
Line 3	Participle embedding *(shrimp-filled)*	Phrase
Line 4	Subordination (adverbial—*when*)	Clause

Rhyme Family

[-imp] *blimp, limp, shrimp, skimp*

Teaching Ideas

Introductory Sharing:	catching and cooking shrimp; ordering shrimp in a restaurant
Vocabulary Targets:	*skimp, serve, shrimp, feast,* "*limp,*" "*shrimp-filled blimp*"
Extension Activity:	Bring in shrimp for the children. Cook, shell, and eat them.

Comments, Observations, and Additional Teaching Ideas

Please don't skimp.   _____

You serve shrimp.   when _____.

I'll feast on shrimp.   _____

This is until I'm limp.   until _____.

I'll become a blimp.   _____.

The blimp is shrimp-filled. a _____ blimp.

Please don't skimp.   Oh, _____

You serve shrimp.   _____!

Chant 76: Skateboard Ramp   Level = M

Chant Model

Kate and Nate like skating camp.
There they skate the skateboard ramp.
Muscles cramp, and shirts get damp.
Oh, Kate and Nate like skating camp!

Syntax Goals

Line 1	Gerund embedding *(skating)*	Phrase
Line 2	Noun embedding *(skateboard)*	Phrase
Line 3	Coordination *(and)*	Clause
Line 4	Gerund embedding *(skating)*	Phrase

Rhyme Families

[-amp] *camp, cramp, damp, ramp*
[-ate] *Kate, Nate, skate*

Teaching Ideas

Introductory Sharing: experiences with skateboarding; skateboard ramps
Vocabulary Targets: *skating camp, skateboard ramp, muscles, cramp, shirts, damp*
Extension Activity: Bring in a skateboard for the children to see. If possible, allow each
child to ride on the skateboard for a short period of time.

Comments, Observations, and Additional Teaching Ideas

Kate and Nate like camp.   _____

It is for skating.   like _____ camp.

There they skate the ramp.   _____

It is for skateboards.   the _____ ramp.

Muscles cramp.   _____,

Shirts get damp.   and _____.

Kate and Nate like camp.   Oh, _____

It is for skating.   _____!

Chant 77: Skiing Free   Level = D

Chant Model

We are kids who love to ski.

Though we slip, we feel so free.

Though we flip, we still shout "Whee!"

Oh, we are kids who love to ski!

Syntax Goals

Line 1	Subordination (relative—*who*)	Clause
Line 2	Subordination (adverbial—*though*)	Clause
Line 3	Subordination (adverbial—*though*)	Clause
Line 4	Subordination (relative—*who*)	Clause

Rhyme Families

[-ee] *free, ski, we, whee*

[-ew] *to, who*

[-ip] *flip, slip*

[-ow] *oh, so, though*

Teaching Ideas

Introductory Sharing: downhill skiing; equipment used; skiing experiences

Vocabulary Targets: *ski, slip, "feel so free," flip, "whee"*

Extension Activity: Show a videotape or pictures of people skiing. Have the children pretend to ski by imitating the actions of the people they see skiing.

Comments, Observations, and Additional Teaching Ideas

We are kids.   _____

We love to ski.   who _____.

We slip.   Though _____,

We feel so free.   we _____.

We flip.   Though _____,

We still shout "Whee!"   we _____!

We are kids.   Oh, _____

We love to ski.   _____!

Chant 78: Skunk Trunk

Level = M

Chant Model

There were skunks inside my trunk.

They had used it for a bunk.

I moved fast, but I was sunk.

Oh, there were skunks inside my trunk!

Syntax Goals

Line 1	Preposition embedding *(inside)*	Phrase
Line 2	Preposition embedding *(for)*	Phrase
Line 3	Coordination *(but)*	Clause
Line 4	Preposition embedding *(inside)*	Phrase

Rhyme Families

[-unk] *bunk, skunk(s), sunk, trunk*

[-y] *I, my*

Teaching Ideas

Introductory Sharing: skunks; the smell of skunks; where skunks live

Vocabulary Targets: *skunk, inside, trunk, bunk, "moved fast," sunk*

Extension Activity: Bring in a stuffed toy skunk; discuss what to do if you see a skunk.

Comments, Observations, and Additional Teaching Ideas

There were skunks.   _____

They were inside my trunk.   inside _____.

They had used it.   _____

It was for a bunk.   for _____.

I moved fast.   _____,

I was sunk.   but _____.

There were skunks.   Oh, _____

They were inside my trunk.   _____!

Chant 79: Slim Jim   Level = M

Chant Model

Jim is slim and very trim.

He spends time inside a gym.

Then he goes to take a swim.

Oh, Jim is slim and very trim!

Syntax Goals

Line 1	Adjective coordination *(and)*	Phrase
Line 2	Preposition embedding *(inside)*	Phrase
Line 3	Infinitive embedding	Phrase
	([in order] to)	
Line 4	Adjective coordination *(and)*	Phrase

Rhyme Family

[-im] *gym, Jim, slim, swim, trim*

Teaching Ideas

Introductory Sharing:	favorite exercise or sporting activities; ways to stay healthy and fit; homophones *Jim* and *gym*
Vocabulary Targets:	slim, trim, "spends time," inside, gym
Extension Activity:	Discuss the importance of exercise, and lead the students in a few minutes of calisthenics.

Comments, Observations, and Additional Teaching Ideas

Jim is slim.

_____

Jim is very trim.

and _____.

He spends time.

_____

The time is inside a gym.

inside _____.

Then he goes.

_____

He takes a swim.

to _____.

Jim is slim.

Oh, _____

Jim is very trim.

_____!

Chant 80: Slow Pace
Level = E

Chant Model

We ran well but lost the race.
We had style but a slow pace.
We are proud of our last place.
Oh, we ran well but lost the race!

Syntax Goals

Line 1	Verb Coordination *(but)*		Phrase
Line 2	Noun coordination *(but)*		Phrase
Line 3	Adjective embedding *(last)*		Phrase
Line 4	Verb coordination *(but)*		Phrase

Rhyme Families

[-ace] *pace, place, race*
[-ow] *oh, slow*

Teaching Ideas

Introductory Sharing: running in races; relay races
Vocabulary Targets: *ran, well, lost, race, style, "slow pace," proud, "last place"*
Extension Activity: Read the story *The Tortoise and the Hare* (1985) by Janet Stevens, New York: Holiday House.

Comments, Observations, and Additional Teaching Ideas

We ran well.

_____

We lost the race.   but _____.

We had style.

_____

We had a slow pace.   but _____.

We are proud of our place.

_____

Our place was last.   our _____ place.

We ran well.   Oh, _____

We lost the race.   _____!

Chant 81: Smelly Toes   Level = E

Chant Model

You have a nose, so you can smell.
Smell a rose, and it smells swell.
Try your toes, and I won't tell.
Oh, you have a nose, so you can smell!

Syntax Goals

Line 1	Subordination (adverbial—*so [that]*)	Clause
Line 2	Coordination *(and)*	Clause
Line 3	Coordination *(and)*	Clause
Line 4	Subordination (adverbial—*so [that]*)	Clause

Rhyme Families

[-el] *smell, swell, tell*
[-ose] *nose, rose, toes*
[-ow] *oh, so*
[-y] *I, try*

Teaching Ideas

Introductory Sharing: things that smell good; things that smell bad

Vocabulary Targets: *smell, rose, swell, tell*

Extension Activity: Bring in bottles of vanilla and vinegar; have the children smell each one and compare the aromas. Discuss their comparisons.

Comments, Observations, and Additional Teaching Ideas

You have a nose.   _____,

You can smell.   so _____.

Smell a rose.   _____,

It smells swell.   and _____.

Try your toes.   _____,

I won't tell.   and _____.

You have a nose.   Oh, _____,

You can smell.   _____!

Chant 82: Snack Attack   Level = D

Chant Model

Ned sneaks snacks while in his bed.

His brain and body both get fed.

As Ned snacks, his books get read.

Oh, Ned sneaks snacks while in
    his bed!

Syntax Goals

Line 1	Subordination (adverbial—*while*)	Clause
Line 2	Noun coordination	Phrase
	(*and* + *both* + *get*)	
Line 3	Subordination (adverbial—*as*)	Clause
Line 4	Subordination (adverbial—*while*)	Clause

Rhyme Families

[-ack] *attack, snack*

[-ed] *bed, fed, Ned, read*

Teaching Ideas

Introductory Sharing: reading in bed; snacking in bed

Vocabulary Targets: *sneak, "snack attack," while, brain, fed, read*

Extension Activity: Have the children role-play and talk about the positions they like to lie
in when reading in bed.

Comments, Observations, and Additional Teaching Ideas

Ned sneaks snacks.   _____

He is in his bed.   while _____.

His brain gets fed.   His _____ and _____

His body gets fed.   both _____.

Ned snacks.   As _____,

His books get read.   _____.

Ned sneaks snacks.   Oh, _____

He is in his bed.   _____!

Chant 83: Snack Packing   Level = E

Chant Model

Jack packs snacks in a backpack.	
His backpack snacks go on his back.	
He hikes beside the railroad track.	
Oh, Jack packs snacks in a backpack!	

Syntax Goals

Line 1	Preposition embedding *(in)*	Phrase
Line 2	Noun embedding *(backpack)*	Phrase
Line 3	Noun embedding *(railroad)*	Phrase
Line 4	Preposition embedding *(in)*	Phrase

Rhyme Families

[-ack] *back, backpack, Jack, pack(s), snack(s), track*

[-ow] *go, oh*

Teaching Ideas

Introductory Sharing:	hiking; backpacking; convenience foods for hikers
Vocabulary Targets:	*packs, backpack, back, hikes, beside, railroad track*
Extension Activity:	Have the children list their favorite snacks. Write the snacks where everyone can see them using a semantic map to group them by "snacks you can pack" and "snacks you can't pack."

Comments, Observations, and Additional Teaching Ideas

Jack packs snacks.   _____

They are in a backpack.   in _____.

His snacks go on his back.   His _____ snacks

Snacks are in the backpack.   go _____.

He hikes beside the track.   _____

The track is for the railroad.   the _____ track.

Jack packs snacks.   Oh, _____

They are in a backpack.   _____!

Chant 84: Snap-Happy Rap   Level = D

Chant Model

Kay and Ray are into rap.
How their toes and fingers snap!
Their noise just stopped the baby's nap.
Oh, Kay and Ray are into rap!

Syntax Goals

Line 1	Noun coordination *(and + are)*	Phrase
Line 2	Noun coordination *(and)*	Phrase
Line 3	Possessive embedding *(baby's)*	Phrase
Line 4	Noun coordination *(and + are)*	Phrase

Rhyme Families

[-ap] *nap, rap, snap*
[-ay] *Kay, Ray*

Teaching Ideas

Introductory Sharing:	rap music; favorite rap singers; waking babies with loud noises
Vocabulary Targets:	*"into," rap, stopped, "snap-happy"*
Extension Activity:	Play a recording of a short rap song; have the children snap their fingers to the rhythm.

Comments, Observations, and Additional Teaching Ideas

Kay is into rap.

_____ and _____

Ray is into rap.

_____ .

How their toes snap!

_____

How their fingers snap!

and _____ !

Their noise just stopped a nap.

_____

The nap was the baby's.

the _____ nap.

Kay is into rap.

Oh, _____

Ray is into rap.

_____ !

Chant 85: Soccer Game   Level = M

Chant Model

Brock played in a soccer game.

His socks slipped when he took aim.

Friends just laughed, then cheered
his name.

Oh, Brock played in a soccer game!

Syntax Goals

Line 1	Noun embedding *(soccer)*	Phrase
Line 2	Subordination (adverbial—*when*)	Clause
Line 3	Verb coordination *(then)*	Phrase
Line 4	Noun embedding *(soccer)*	Phrase

Rhyme Families

[-ame] *aim, game, name*

[-en] *then, when*

[-ock] *Brock, sock(s)*

Teaching Ideas

Introductory Sharing: experiences playing soccer

Vocabulary Targets: *soccer, slipped, aim, cheered, name*

Extension Activity: Bring in a soccer ball for the children to see and use. Show a picture
or videotape of children playing soccer.

Comments, Observations, and Additional Teaching Ideas

Brock played in a game.   _____

It was called soccer.   a _____ game.

His socks slipped.   _____

He took aim.   when _____.

Friends just laughed.   _____,

Friends cheered his name.   then _____.

Brock played in a game.   Oh, _____

It was called soccer.   _____!

Chant 86: Spiked Hair   Level = M

Chant Model

Harry is a scary child.

Spiked white hair makes him look wild.

Let's wait and watch while it gets styled.

Oh, Harry is a scary child!

Syntax Goals

Line 1	Adjective embedding *(scary)*	Phrase
Line 2	Adjective embedding *(white)*	Phrase
Line 3	Subordination (adverbial—*while*)	Clause
Line 4	Adjective embedding *(scary)*	Phrase

Rhyme Families

[-ary] *Harry, scary*

[-ild] *child, styled, wild*

Teaching Ideas

Introductory Sharing: favorite hairstyles; hairstyle fads

Vocabulary Targets: *scary, child, "spiked hair," wild, styled*

Extension Activity: Have the children find and cut out wild hairstyles from magazines. Encourage each child to write or tell a story about the wild hairstyle he or she finds.

Comments, Observations, and Additional Teaching Ideas

Harry is a child.   _____

He is scary.   a _____ child.

Spiked hair makes him   Spiked _____ hair
    look wild.

His hair is white.   makes _____.

Let's wait and watch.   _____

It gets styled.   while _____.

Harry is a child.   Oh, _____

He is scary.   _____!

213

Chant 87: Stan the Man   Level = M

Chant Model

Stan is a man who likes to run.

He runs in the rain and runs in the sun.

He runs for fun but has never won.

Oh, Stan is a man who likes to run!

Syntax Goals

Line 1	Subordination (relative—*who*)	Clause
Line 2	Verb coordination *(and)*	Phrase
Line 3	Verb coordination *(but)*	Phrase
Line 4	Subordination (relative—*who*)	Clause

Rhyme Families

[-an] *man, Stan*

[-ew] *to, who*

[-un] *fun, run, sun, won*

Teaching Ideas

Introductory Sharing: running in races; running as exercise; parents who run

Vocabulary Targets: *man, won, "for fun"*

Extension Activity: Show a picture of marathon runners; demonstrate jogging or have the children role-play jogging in a race.

Comments, Observations, and Additional Teaching Ideas

Stan is a man.   _____

He likes to run.   who _____.

He runs in the rain.   _____

He runs in the sun.   and _____.

He runs for fun.   _____

He has never won.   but _____.

Stan is a man.   Oh, _____

He likes to run.   _____!

Chant 88: Sugar Blues   Level = M

Chant Model

Too much sugar is bad for you.

You first feel buzzy and then feel blue.

If you eat less sugar, you feel brand new.

Oh, too much sugar is bad for you!

Syntax Goals

Line 1	Adjective embedding *(too much)*	Phrase
Line 2	Verb coordination *(and)*	Phrase
Line 3	Subordination (adverbial—*if*)	Clause
Line 4	Adjective embedding *(too much)*	Phrase

Rhyme Family

[-ew] *blue, new, too, you*

Teaching Ideas

Introductory Sharing: foods that are high in sugar; the effects of eating too much sugar

Vocabulary Targets: *sugar, "bad for you," first, "feel buzzy," "feel blue," less, "feel brand new"*

Extension Activity: Bring treats to class that are low in sugar. Discuss the importance of choosing low-sugar snacks as often as possible. Allow each child to have a snack.

Comments, Observations, and Additional Teaching Ideas

Sugar is bad for you.   Too much _____

The sugar is too much.   is _____.

You first feel buzzy.   _____

You then feel blue.   and _____.

Eat less sugar.   If _____,

You feel brand new.   you _____.

Sugar is bad for you.   Oh, _____

The sugar is too much.   _____!

Chant 89: Summertime   Level = E

Chant Model

Paulo likes summer the best of all.

Grass grows green, and corn grows tall.

Days are warm, so he plays ball.

Oh, Paulo likes summer the best of all!

Syntax Goals

Line 1	Adverb embedding *(the best of all)*	Phrase
Line 2	Coordination *(and)*	Clause
Line 3	Coordination *(so)*	Clause
Line 4	Adverb embedding *(the best of all)*	Phrase

Rhyme Families

[-awl] *all, ball, tall*

[-ow] *oh, grow(s), Paulo, so*

Teaching Ideas

Introductory Sharing: summer weather; summer plants; summer activities

Vocabulary Targets: *best, grows, corn, tall, warm, "plays ball," summertime*

Extension Activity: Have each child identify and talk about his or her favorite summer activity. Allow each child to draw a picture of himself or herself participating in the activity.

Comments, Observations, and Additional Teaching Ideas

Paulo likes summer. _____

It is the best of all. the best _____.

Grass grows green. _____,

Corn grows tall. and _____.

Days are warm. _____,

He plays ball. so _____.

Paulo likes summer. Oh, _____

It is the best of all. _____!

Chant 90: Surfing   Level = D

Chant Model   ### Syntax Goals

Dave craves waves that he can ride.	Line 1	Subordination (relative—*that*)	Clause
Down he shoots and rides inside.	Line 2	Verb coordination *(and)*	Phrase
In the curl he tries to hide.	Line 3	Preposition embedding *(in)*	Phrase
Oh, Dave craves waves that he can ride!	Line 4	Subordination (relative—*that*)	Clause

Rhyme Families

[-ave] *crave(s), Dave, wave(s)*

[-ide] *hide, inside, ride*

Teaching Ideas

Introductory Sharing: surfing experiences; watching surfers on TV; surfing equipment

Vocabulary Targets: *surfing, craves, waves, ride, down, "shoots," inside, curl, tries, hide*

Extension Activity: Show a picture or videotape of a person surfing. Encourage the children to role-play the motions of surfing.

Comments, Observations, and Additional Teaching Ideas

Dave craves waves. _____

He can ride them. that _____.

Down he shoots. _____

He rides inside. and _____.

He tries to hide. In _____

It is in the curl. _____.

Dave craves waves. Oh, _____

He can ride them. _____!

Chant 91: Swim Song   Level = M

Chant Model

Let's dive in and have a swim.

Swimming keeps us fit and trim.

If we swim, we will stay slim.

Oh, let's dive in and have a swim!

Syntax Goals

Line 1	Verb coordination *(and)*	Phrase
Line 2	Adjective coordination *(and)*	Phrase
Line 3	Subordination (adverbial—*if*)	Clause
Line 4	Verb coordination *(and)*	Phrase

Rhyme Family

[-im] *slim, swim, trim*

Teaching Ideas

Introductory Sharing: experiences diving and swimming

Vocabulary Targets: *dive, swim, fit, trim, slim*

Extension Activity: Show a picture or videotape of people diving and swimming. Have the children imitate swimming strokes and diving positions.

Comments, Observations, and Additional Teaching Ideas

Let's dive in.   _____

Let's have a swim.   and _____.

Swimming keeps us fit.   _____

Swimming keeps us trim.   _____ and _____.

We swim.   If _____,

We will stay slim.   _____.

Let's dive in.   Oh, _____

Let's have a swim.   _____!

Chant 92: Ted's Bed   Level = M

Chant Model

Ted is in bed when he makes shrieks.

Something lurks between his sheets.

Ted leaps up, and out it peeks.

Oh, Ted is in bed when he
makes shrieks!

Syntax Goals

Line 1	Subordination (adverbial—*when*)	Clause
Line 2	Preposition embedding *(between)*	Phrase
Line 3	Coordination *(and)*	Clause
Line 4	Subordination (adverbial—*when*)	Clause

Rhyme Families

[-eaks] *peeks, shrieks*

[-ed] *bed, Ted*

Teaching Ideas

Introductory Sharing:	experiences with pets hiding under bed covers
Vocabulary Targets:	*shrieks, lurks, between, sheets, "leaps up," peeks*
Extension Activity:	Have the children role-play crawling into bed, feeling something, and then leaping out and shrieking, "What is that?"

Comments, Observations, and Additional Teaching Ideas

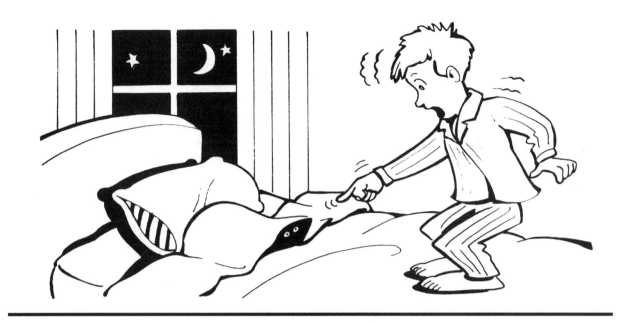

Ted is in bed. _____

He makes shrieks. when _____.

Something lurks. _____

It is between his sheets. between _____.

Ted leaps up. _____,

Out it peeks. and _____.

Ted is in bed. Oh, _____

He makes shrieks. _____!

Chant 93: Tennis Fan   Level = M

Chant Model

Dennis is a tennis fan.
He plays tennis when he can.
The summer sun gives him a tan.
Oh, Dennis is a tennis fan!

Syntax Goals

Line 1	Noun embedding *(tennis)*	Phrase
Line 2	Subordination (adverbial—*when)*	Clause
Line 3	Noun embedding *(summer)*	Phrase
Line 4	Noun embedding *(tennis)*	Phrase

Rhyme Families

[-an] *can, fan, tan*
[-ennis] *Dennis, tennis*

Teaching Ideas

Introductory Sharing:	experiences watching or playing tennis
Vocabulary Targets:	tennis, fan, tan
Extension Activity:	Bring in a tennis racket and ball. Talk about other sports that use a racket.

Comments, Observations, and Additional Teaching Ideas

Dennis is a fan.   _____

He likes tennis.   a _____ fan.

He plays tennis.   _____

He can play.   when _____.

The sun gives him a tan.   The _____ sun

The sun is in summer.   gives _____.

Dennis is a fan.   Oh, _____

He likes tennis.   _____!

Chant 94: Ten-Speed Mike   Level = M

Chant Model

Mike is a kid who wants a bike.

He's 10 years old but rides a trike.

A ten-speed bike is what he'd like.

Oh, Mike is a kid who wants a bike!

Syntax Goals

Line 1	Subordination (relative—*who*)	Clause
Line 2	Verb coordination *(but)*	Phrase
Line 3	Noun embedding *(ten-speed)*	Phrase
Line 4	Subordination (relative—*who*)	Clause

Rhyme Family

[-ike] *bike, like, Mike, trike*

Teaching Ideas

Introductory Sharing: bicycles and tricycles; how to use the different speeds; bike racing

Vocabulary Targets: *trike, ten-speed bike*

Extension Activity: Show pictures of people riding different types of bikes. Have the children draw pictures of bicycles and tricycles. Talk about the differences between the various types of bikes.

Comments, Observations, and Additional Teaching Ideas

Mike is a kid. _____

He wants a bike. who _____.

He's 10 years old. _____

He rides a trike. but _____.

A bike is what he'd like. A _____ bike

The bike is a ten-speed. _____.

Mike is a kid. Oh, _____

He wants a bike. _____!

Chant 95: Tori's Story   Level = M

Chant Model

Tori read a gory book.

The story scared her, so don't look.

There's a crook named Captain Hook.

Oh, Tori read a gory book!

Syntax Goals

Line 1	Adjective embedding *(gory)*	Phrase
Line 2	Coordination *(so)*	Clause
Line 3	Participle embedding *(named)*	Phrase
Line 4	Adjective embedding *(gory)*	Phrase

Rhyme Families

[-ook] *crook, Hook, look, storybook*

[-ory] *gory, story, Tori*

[-ow] *oh, so*

Teaching Ideas

Introductory Sharing:	favorite storybooks; scary stories
Vocabulary Targets:	*gory, scared, crook, named, Captain Hook*
Extension Activity:	Read the book *Peter Pan* (1983) by James Matthew Barrie, New York: Random Books.

Comments, Observations, and Additional Teaching Ideas

Tori read a book.   _____

The book was gory.   a _____.

The story scared her.   _____,

Don't look.   so _____.

There's a crook.   _____

He is named Captain Hook.   named _____.

Tori read a book.   Oh, _____

The book was gory.   _____!

Chant 96: Water Slide Clyde   Level = M

Chant Model

Clyde just had a super ride.
He swooped down the water slide.
His lost suit means he must hide.
Oh, Clyde just had a super ride!

Syntax Goals

Line 1	Adjective embedding *(super)*		Phrase
Line 2	Noun embedding *(water)*		Phrase
Line 3	Subordination (nominal—*[that]*)		Clause
Line 4	Adjective embedding *(super)*		Phrase

Rhyme Family

[-ide] *Clyde, hide, ride, slide*

Teaching Ideas

Introductory Sharing: experiences with riding water slides

Vocabulary Targets: *super, ride, "swooped down," water slide, lost, suit, hide*

Extension Activity: Discuss the children's favorite water slide rides. Have the children draw pictures of people sliding down a water slide.

Comments, Observations, and Additional Teaching Ideas

Clyde just had a ride.   _____

It was super.   a _____ ride.

He swooped down the slide.   _____

The slide was for water.   the _____ slide.

His lost suit means something. _____

He must hide.   he _____ .

Clyde just had a ride.   Oh, _____

It was super.   _____!

233

Chant 97: Whiz Kid   Level = D

Chant Model

I know a girl whose name is Liz.

Her high scores top every quiz.

With computers, she's a whiz.

Oh, I know a girl whose name is Liz!

Syntax Goals

Line 1	Subordination (relative—*whose*)	Clause
Line 2	Adjective embedding *(high)*	Phrase
Line 3	Preposition embedding *(with)*	Phrase
Line 4	Subordination (relative—*whose*)	Clause

Rhyme Families

[-is] *is, Liz, quiz, whiz*

[-ow] *know, oh*

[-y] *high, I*

Teaching Ideas

Introductory Sharing: taking quizzes; quiz scores; computers; being really good at something

Vocabulary Targets: "high scores," "top," quiz, computers, "whiz kid"

Extension Activity: Talk about activities or classes the students are really good at.

Comments, Observations, and Additional Teaching Ideas

I know a girl.   _____

Her name is Liz.   whose _____.

Her scores top every quiz.   Her _____ scores

Her scores are high.   _____.

She's a whiz.   With _____,

This is with computers.   _____.

I know a girl.   Oh, _____

Her name is Liz.   _____!

Chant 98: Will's Thrill   Level = M

Chant Model

> Will is a lad who had a thrill.
>
> His red sled sped down a hill.
>
> Off Will flew when it stopped still.
>
> Oh, Will is a lad who had a thrill!

Syntax Goals

Line 1	Subordination (relative—*who*)	Clause
Line 2	Adjective embedding *(red)*	Phrase
Line 3	Subordination (adverbial—*when*)	Clause
Line 4	Subordination (relative—*who*)	Clause

Rhyme Families

[-ad] *had, lad*

[-ed] *red, sled, sped*

[-ew] *flew, who*

[-ill] *hill, still, thrill, Will*

Teaching Ideas

Introductory Sharing:	sleds; hills for sledding
Vocabulary Targets:	*lad, thrill, sled, sped, flew, "stopped still"*
Extension Activity:	Talk about different materials students could use to create a home-made sled (e.g., cardboard, plastic tray, garbage can lid).

Comments, Observations, and Additional Teaching Ideas

Will is a lad.   _____

He had a thrill.   who _____.

His sled sped down a hill.   His _____ sled

His sled was red.   _____.

Off Will flew.   _____

It stopped still.   when _____.

Will is a lad.   Oh, _____

He had a thrill.   _____!

Chant 99: Win or Lose   Level = E

Chant Model

> Step right up, and hear the news.
> You can win, or you can lose.
> You can smile or choose the blues.
> Oh, step right up, and hear the news!

Syntax Goals

Line 1	Coordination *(and)*	Clause
Line 2	Coordination *(or)*	Clause
Line 3	Verb coordination *(or)*	Phrase
Line 4	Coordination *(and)*	Clause

Rhyme Family

[-ooze] *blues, choose, lose, news*

Teaching Ideas

Introductory Sharing: successes in school, sports, and other activities
Vocabulary Targets: *"step right up," "hear the news," "win or lose," "choose the blues"*
Extension Activity: Have each child share something he or she does well.

Comments, Observations, and Additional Teaching Ideas

Step right up.	_____,
Hear the news.	and _____.
You can win.	_____,
You can lose.	or _____.
You can smile.	_____
You can choose the blues.	or _____.
Step right up.	Oh, _____,
Hear the news.	_____!

Chant 100: Zack and Zaney   Level = D

Chant Model

Zack bit a dog that bit him back.

Zack chased Zaney around the track.

The race changed pace as
  Zaney chased Zack.

Oh, Zack bit a dog that bit him back!

Syntax Goals

Line 1	Subordination (relative—*that*)	Clause
Line 2	Preposition embedding *(around)*	Phrase
Line 3	Subordination (adverbial—*as*)	Clause
Line 4	Subordination (relative—*that*)	Clause

Rhyme Families

[-ace] *chase(d), pace, race, chase(d)*

[-ack] *back, track, Zack*

Teaching Ideas

Introductory Sharing: experiences with a biting dog

Vocabulary Targets: *bit, "bit him back," around, track, "changed pace," chased*

Extension Activity: Discuss the local leash laws and why they are important. Talk about what to do when meeting an unfamiliar or unleashed dog.

Comments, Observations, and Additional Teaching Ideas

Zack bit a dog.   _____

It bit him back.   that _____.

Zack chased Zaney.   _____

It was around the track.   around _____.

The race changed pace.   _____,

Zaney chased Zack.   as _____.

Zack bit a dog.   Oh, _____

It bit him back.   _____!

Appendixes

Example Long-Term Goals

The student will:

1. Comprehend and produce sentences with coordinated phrases in spoken and/or written language.

2. Comprehend and produce sentences with embedded phrases in spoken and/or written language.

3. Comprehend and produce sentences with coordinated clauses in spoken and/or written language.

4. Comprehend and produce sentences with subordinated clauses in spoken and/or written language.

5. Identify rhyming words.

Example Short-Term Objectives

The student will:

1. Use coordinated adjective phrases in sentences when retelling a story.

2. Use embedded adverb phrases in sentences when writing a book report.

3. Coordinate clauses using adversative conjunctions *(for example, but)* when telling a personal experience story.

4. Use adverbial clauses *(if)* when providing instructions for accomplishing a task to another student.

5. Use nominal clauses *(that)* when writing dialogue for a created story.

6. Use relative clauses *(who)* when writing a biography for a classroom assignment.

7. Identify phonemes in the word-final position.

A Famous Story #1

Jack went up the hill.

Jill went up the hill.

They went to fetch a pail.

Water was in the pail.

Jack fell down.

He broke his crown.

Jill came tumbling after him.

Jack and Jill

Jack and Jill went up the hill

To fetch a pail of water.

Jack fell down and broke his crown,

And Jill came tumbling after.

A Famous Story #2

The spider climbed up
the water spout.

The spider was itsy-bitsy.

The _____ spider

_____.

Down came the rain.

It washed the spider out.

_____

and _____.

Out came the sun.

It dried up all the rain.

_____

and _____.

The spider climbed up
the spout again.

The spider was itsy-bitsy.

So, _____

_____!

Recording Form for Syntactic Structures

Student Name: _____

Indicate the date, chant number, and student's level of performance for the chant exercise in the columns to the right of the syntactic structure. Use the following scale for level of performance:

FD— *Full dependence* on adult model for successful sentence combining

ES— Independent chant problem solving with *extensive support* from adult

MS— Independent chant problem solving with *minimal support* from adult

I— *Independent* chant problem solving

FP— Independent chant problem solving and *full participation* in oral/choral chanting using title or picture cue only

Phrase Coordination					
Adjective					
and					
but					
or					
Noun					
and					
and + SV*					
but					
or					
Verb					
and					
but					
or					
then					

* SV = subject/verb agreement

Phrase Embedding					
Adjective					
Adverb					
-ly					
phrase					
Appositive					
noun					
adjective					
Gerund					
Infinitive					
Noun					
Participle					
Possessive					
Preposition					
along					
around					
at					
because of					
behind					
beneath					
between					
beyond					
by					

Phrase Embedding				
Phrase Embedding: Preposition—*Continued*				
for				
from				
in				
inside				
like				
of				
off				
on				
till				
to				
until				
up				
upon				
with				
without				
Clause Coordination				
and				
but				
or				
so				

Clause Subordination					
Adverbial					
after					
as					
because					
if					
so [that]					
though					
until					
when					
where					
while					
Nominal					
that					
[that]					
what					
Relative					
that					
[that]					
which					
who					
whose					

References

Adams, M.J., Foorman, B.R., Lundberg, I., and Beeler, T. (1998). *Phonemic awareness in young children: A classroom curriculum.* Baltimore: Brookes.

Ball, E., and Blachman, B. (1988). Phoneme segmentation training: Effect on reading readiness. *Annals of Dyslexia, 38,* 208–225.

Buchoff, R. (1994). Joyful voices: Facilitating language growth through the rhythmic response to chants. *Young Children, 49,* 26–30.

Carrow-Woolfolk, E. (1985). *Test for auditory comprehension of language* (Rev. ed.). Austin, TX: Pro-Ed.

Carter, D.A. (1995). *Love bugs.* New York: Simon and Schuster.

Combs, W.E. (1977). Sentence combining practice: Do gains in judgments of writing 'quality' persist? *Journal of Educational Research, 70,* 318–321.

Gallimore, R., and Tharp, R. (1990). Teaching mind in society: Teaching, schooling, and literate discourse. In L.C. Moll (Ed.), *Vygotsky and education* (pp. 175–205). New York: Press Syndicate of the University of Cambridge.

Gilbertson, M., and Bramlett, R.K. (1998). Phonological awareness screening to identify at-risk readers: Implications for practitioners. *Language, Speech, and Hearing Services in Schools, 29,* 109–116.

Goldsworthy, C.L. (1998). *Sourcebook of phonological awareness activities: Children's classic literature.* San Diego, CA: Singular.

Hammill, D.D., and Newcomer, P.L. (1997). *Test of language development—Intermediate* (3rd ed.). Austin, TX: Pro-Ed.

Hillocks, G., Jr. (1986). *Research on written composition: New directions for teaching.* Urbana, IL: ERIC Clearinghouse on Reading and Communication Skills and the National Conference on Research in English. (ERIC Document Reproduction Service No. 265 552)

Hunt, K.W. (1965). *Grammatical structures written at three grade levels.* (NCTE Research Report No. 3). Urbana, IL: National Council of Teachers of English. (ERIC Document Reproduction Service No. 113 735)

Hunt, K.W. (1977). Early-blooming and late-blooming syntactic structures. In C.R. Cooper and L. O'Dell (Eds.), *Evaluating writing: Describing, measuring, judging.* Urbana, IL: National Council of Teachers of English.

IRA board issues position statement on phonemic awareness. (1998, June/July). *Reading Today, 15*(6), 26.

Krashen, S.D. (1984). *Writing: Research, theory, and applications.* Oxford: Pergamon Press.

Lawlor, J. (1983). Sentence combining: A sequence for instruction. *Elementary School Journal, 84,* 53–62.

Lee, L. (1974). *Developmental sentence analysis.* Evanston, IL: Northwestern University Press.

Lindamood, C., and Lindamood, P. (1971). *Lindamood auditory conceptualization test.* Austin, TX: Pro-Ed.

Loban, W. (1976). *Language development: Kindergarten through grade 12.* Urbana, IL: National Council of Teachers of English.

Majsterek, D.J., and Ellenwood, A.E. (1995). Phonological awareness and beginning reading: Evaluation of a school-based screening procedure. *Journal of Learning Disabilities, 28*(7), 449–456.

McCracken, M.J., and McCracken, R.A. (1986). *Stories, songs and poetry to teach reading and writing: Literacy through language.* Chicago: American Library Association.

McFadden, T.U. (1998). Sounds and stories: Teaching phonemic awareness in interactions around text. *American Journal of Speech-Language Pathology, 7*(2), 5–13.

Miller, J., and Chapman, R. (1991). *SALT: A computer program for the systematic analysis of language transcripts* [Computer software]. Madison, WI: Language Analysis Laboratory, Waisman Center, University of Wisconsin.

Moffett, J. (1992). *Detecting growth in language.* Portsmouth, NH: Heinemann-Boynton/Cook.

Newcomer, P.L., and Hammill, D.D. (1997). *Test of language development—Primary* (3rd ed.). Austin, TX: Pro-Ed.

Norton, D.E. (1991). *Through the eyes of a child.* New York: Merrill.

O'Donnell, R.C., Griffin, W.J., and Norris, R.C. (1967). *Syntax of kindergarten and elementary school children—A transformational analysis.* Urbana, IL: National Council of Teachers of English. (ERIC Document Reproduction Service No. 017 508)

Retherford, K. (1993). *Guide to analysis of language transcripts* (2nd ed.). Eau Claire, WI: Thinking Publications.

Sawyer, D. (1987). *Test of awareness of language segments.* Austin, TX: Pro-Ed.

Scott, C.M. (1988a). Producing complex sentences. *Topics in Language Disorders, 8*(2), 44–62.

Scott, C.M. (1988b). Spoken and written syntax. In M.A. Nippold (Ed.), *Later language development* (pp. 49–95). Boston: College-Hill.

Stein, J. (Ed.). (1985). *The Random House rhyming dictionary.* New York: Random House.

Stone, B.H., Merritt, D.D., and Cherkes-Julkowski, M. (1998). Language and reading: Phonological connections. In D.D. Merritt and B. Culatta (Eds.), *Language intervention in the classroom* (pp. 363–408). San Diego, CA: Singular.

Strong, C. (1998). *Strong narrative assessment procedure (SNAP).* Eau Claire, WI: Thinking Publications.

Strong, W. (1986). *Creative approaches to sentence combining.* Urbana, IL: ERIC Clearinghouse on Reading and Communication Skills and the National Council of Teachers of English.

Strong, W., and Strong, C.J. (1994, August). *Vygotsky revisited: How sentence combining works.* Paper presented at the Global Conversations on Language and Literacy Conference sponsored by NCTE, NWP, DoDDS, and NATE, Oxford, England.

Torgesen, J.K., and Bryant, B.R. (1994). *Test of phonological awareness.* Austin, TX: Pro-Ed.

Torgesen, J.K., Wagner, R.K., and Rashotte, C. (1994). Longitudinal studies of phonological processing and reading. *Journal of Learning Disabilities, 27,* 276–286.

Vygotsky, L. (1962). *Thought and language.* Cambridge, MA: MIT Press.

Vygotsky, L. (1978). *Mind in society.* Cambridge, MA: Harvard University Press.

Wilkinson, P.A., and Patty, D. (1993). The effects of sentence combining on the reading comprehension of fourth grade students. *Research in the Teaching of English, 27*(1), 104–125.

Indexes

Level: Easy (E)

Chant #	Title	Line	Syntactic Structures	Context
3	Bareback Mac	1, 4	Preposition embedding *(to)*	Phrase
		2	Noun embedding *(midnight)*	Phrase
		3	Verb coordination *(and)*	Phrase
9	Chanting	1, 4	Adverb embedding *(line by line)*	Phrase
		2	Subordination (adverbial—*when*)	Clause
		3	Verb coordination *(and)*	Phrase
24	Gluey Stew	1, 4	Subordination (relative—*that*)	Clause
		2	Coordination *(and)*	Clause
		3	Coordination *(and)*	Clause
33	Irv's Curve	1, 4	Noun coordination *(and)*	Phrase
		2	Participle embedding *(swooping)*	Phrase
		3	Verb coordination *(and)*	Phrase
53	Numb Thumb	1, 4	Subordination (relative—*that*)	Clause
		2	Verb coordination *(and)*	Phrase
		3	Adjective coordination *(and)*	Phrase
54	Park Shark	1, 4	Preposition embedding *(at)*	Phrase
		2	Preposition embedding *(till)*	Phrase
		3	Adjective embedding *(scary)*	Phrase
55	Pat's Cats	1, 4	Coordination *(and)*	Clause
		2	Coordination *(and)*	Clause
		3	Preposition embedding *(like)*	Phrase
59	Popcorn	1, 4	Adjective embedding *(favorite)*	Phrase
		2	Adjective embedding *(friendly)*	Phrase
		3	Adjective coordination *(or)*	Phrase
60	Portland Fog	1, 4	Noun coordination *(and)*	Phrase
		2	Subordination (adverbial—*when*)	Clause
		3	Noun coordination *(or)*	Phrase

Level: Easy (E)—*Continued*

Chant #	Title	Line	Syntactic Structures	Context
62	Red Ants	1, 4	Noun embedding *(pet)*	Phrase
		2	Preposition embedding *(in)*	Phrase
		3	Noun coordination *(and)*	Phrase
64	Rice Pudding	1, 4	Coordination *(and)*	Clause
		2	Coordination *(and)*	Clause
		3	Coordination *(and)*	Clause
80	Slow Pace	1, 4	Verb coordination *(but)*	Phrase
		2	Noun coordination *(but)*	Phrase
		3	Adjective embedding *(last)*	Phrase
81	Smelly Toes	1, 4	Subordination (adverbial—*so [that]*)	Clause
		2	Coordination *(and)*	Clause
		3	Coordination *(and)*	Clause
83	Snack Packing	1, 4	Preposition embedding *(in)*	Phrase
		2	Noun embedding *(backpack)*	Phrase
		3	Noun embedding *(railroad)*	Phrase
89	Summertime	1, 4	Adverb embedding *(the best of all)*	Phrase
		2	Coordination *(and)*	Clause
		3	Coordination *(so)*	Clause
99	Win or Lose	1, 4	Coordination *(and)*	Clause
		2	Coordination *(or)*	Clause
		3	Verb coordination *(or)*	Phrase

Level: Moderate (M)

Chant #	Title	Line	Syntactic Structures	Context
1	Back Flip	1, 4	Adjective embedding *(new)*	Phrase
		2	Verb coordination *(or)*	Phrase
		3	Subordination (adverbial—*if*)	Clause
4	Big Sneeze	1, 4	Preposition embedding *(behind)*	Phrase
		2	Verb coordination *(and)*	Phrase
		3	Adverb embedding *(worst of all)*	Phrase
5	Blake Snores	1, 4	Preposition embedding *(until)*	Phrase
		2	Possessive embedding *(Blake's)*	Phrase
		3	Preposition embedding *(with)*	Phrase
6	Burgers and Fries	1, 4	Coordination *(and)*	Clause
		2	Preposition embedding *(of)*	Phrase
		3	Preposition embedding *(for)*	Phrase
8	Camping	1, 4	Preposition embedding *(because of)*	Phrase
		2	Noun embedding *(water)*	Phrase
		3	Adverb embedding *(best of all)*	Phrase
10	Chuck's Truck	1, 4	Appositive noun embedding *(Chuck)*	Phrase
		2	Noun embedding *(pickup)*	Phrase
		3	Adjective embedding *(knee-deep)*	Phrase
14	Dirt Bikes	1, 4	Preposition embedding *(in)*	Phrase
		2	Noun coordination *(and)*	Phrase
		3	Noun embedding *(doctor)*	Phrase
15	Dog Bath	1, 4	Noun coordination *(and + smell)*	Phrase
		2	Verb coordination *(and)*	Phrase
		3	Coordination *(and)*	Clause
17	Dream Team	1, 4	Subordination (relative—*that*)	Clause
		2	Subordination (adverbial—*after*)	Clause
		3	Verb coordination *(and)*	Phrase

Level: Moderate (M)—*Continued*

Chant #	Title	Line	Syntactic Structures	Context
18	Fall Colors	1, 4	Subordination (adverbial—*as*)	Clause
		2	Gerund embedding *(swimming)*	Phrase
		3	Adjective embedding *(football)*	Phrase
19	Floyd the Flea	1, 4	Subordination (relative—*[that]*)	Clause
		2	Preposition embedding *(upon)*	Phrase
		3	Preposition embedding *(for)*	Phrase
20	Flying Free	1, 4	Preposition embedding *(at)*	Phrase
		2	Preposition embedding *(beyond)*	Phrase
		3	Adjective embedding *(free)*	Phrase
23	Ghost Sounds	1, 4	Preposition embedding *(in)*	Phrase
		2	Subordination (adverbial—*as*)	Clause
		3	Preposition embedding *(up)*	Phrase
27	Halloween Fun	1, 4	Noun coordination *(or)*	Phrase
		2	Noun coordination *(and)*	Phrase
		3	Subordination (relative—*[that]*)	Clause
28	Hear the Night	1, 4	Coordination *(and)*	Clause
		2	Preposition embedding *(in)*	Phrase
		3	Subordination (adverbial—*as*)	Clause
29	Hiking	1, 4	Noun coordination *(and)*	Phrase
		2	Coordination *(but)*	Clause
		3	Adjective embedding *(wet)*	Phrase
30	Hockey	1, 4	Noun embedding *(winter)*	Phrase
		2	Adjective embedding *(icy)*	Phrase
		3	Appositive adjective embedding *(tall and short)*	Phrase
32	Hot Dogs	1, 4	Adjective embedding *(cold)*	Phrase
		2	Preposition embedding *(on)*	Phrase
		3	Coordination *(and)*	Clause
34	Jane's Sprain	1, 4	Preposition embedding *(in)*	Phrase
		2	Verb coordination *(and)*	Phrase
		3	Adverb embedding *(while)*	Phrase

266

Level: Moderate (M)—*Continued*

Chant #	Title	Line	Syntactic Structures	Context
35	Jerry's Goof	1, 4	Adjective embedding *(giant)*	Phrase
		2	Preposition embedding *(off)*	Phrase
		3	Subordination (adverbial—*if*)	Clause
36	Joel's Goal	1, 4	Preposition embedding *(with)*	Phrase
		2	Noun coordination *(and)*	Phrase
		3	Verb coordination *(and)*	Phrase
38	Jungle Jim	1, 4	Possessive embedding *(friend's)*	Phrase
		2	Preposition embedding *(beneath)*	Phrase
		3	Subordination (relative—*that*)	Clause
39	Kate Skates	1, 4	Verb coordination *(then)*	Phrase
		2	Coordination *(but)*	Clause
		3	Coordination *(and)*	Clause
41	Kate's Lunch	1, 4	Preposition embedding *(from off)*	Phrase
		2	Subordination (nominal—*that*)	Clause
		3	Preposition embedding *(with)*	Phrase
42	Kick the Can	1, 4	Subordination (adverbial—*if*)	Clause
		2	Coordination *(and)*	Clause
		3	Participle embedding *(kicking)*	Phrase
43	Lime Slime	1, 4	Subordination (adverbial—*when*)	Clause
		2	Adverb embedding *(most anytime)*	Phrase
		3	Subordination (relative—*that*)	Clause
44	Lucille Seal	1, 4	Preposition embedding *(like)*	Phrase
		2	Infinitive embedding *([in order] to)*	Phrase
		3	Coordination *(or)*	Clause
48	Mona the Mouse	1, 4	Subordination (relative—*that*)	Clause
		2	Subordination (adverbial—*when*)	Clause
		3	Preposition embedding *(without)*	Phrase
50	Nachos	1, 4	Preposition embedding *(with)*	Phrase
		2	Preposition embedding *(like)*	Phrase
		3	Subordination (nominal—*[that]*)	Clause

267

Level: Moderate (M)—*Continued*

Chant #	Title	Line	Syntactic Structures	Context
51	Nate the Skater	1, 4	Preposition embedding *(on)*	Phrase
		2	Noun coordination *(and + feel)*	Phrase
		3	Preposition embedding (by)	Phrase
56	Pesky Guest	1, 4	Subordination (nominal—*that*)	Clause
		2	Preposition embedding *(from)*	Phrase
		3	Preposition embedding *(like)*	Phrase
57	Pet Hen	1, 4	Noun coordination *(and + have)*	Phrase
		2	Subordination (relative—*that*)	Clause
		3	Adjective embedding *(cute)*	Phrase
68	Rollerblade Wade	1, 4	Noun coordination *(and)*	Phrase
		2	Subordination (nominal—*that*)	Clause
		3	Noun coordination *(and)*	Phrase
70	Rude Dude	1, 4	Subordination (relative—*who*)	Clause
		2	Verb coordination *(then)*	Phrase
		3	Adjective embedding *(bad)*	Phrase
72	School Is Cool	1, 4	Subordination (adverbial—*because*)	Clause
		2	Adjective embedding *(golden)*	Phrase
		3	Adjective coordination *(and)*	Phrase
76	Skateboard Ramp	1, 4	Gerund embedding *(skating)*	Phrase
		2	Noun embedding *(skateboard)*	Phrase
		3	Coordination *(and)*	Clause
78	Skunk Trunk	1, 4	Preposition embedding *(inside)*	Phrase
		2	Preposition embedding *(for)*	Phrase
		3	Coordination *(but)*	Clause
79	Slim Jim	1, 4	Adjective coordination *(and)*	Phrase
		2	Preposition embedding *(inside)*	Phrase
		3	Infinitive embedding *([in order] to)*	Phrase
85	Soccer Game	1, 4	Noun embedding *(soccer)*	Phrase
		2	Subordination (adverbial—*when*)	Clause
		3	Verb coordination *(then)*	Phrase

Chant #	Title	Line	Syntactic Structures	Context
86	Spiked Hair	1, 4	Adjective embedding *(scary)*	Phrase
		2	Adjective embedding *(white)*	Phrase
		3	Subordination (adverbial—*while*)	Clause
87	Stan the Man	1, 4	Subordination (relative—*who*)	Clause
		2	Verb coordination *(and)*	Phrase
		3	Verb coordination *(but)*	Phrase
88	Sugar Blues	1, 4	Adjective embedding *(too much)*	Phrase
		2	Verb coordination *(and)*	Phrase
		3	Subordination (adverbial—*if*)	Phrase
91	Swim Song	1, 4	Verb coordination *(and)*	Phrase
		2	Adjective coordination *(and)*	Phrase
		3	Subordination (adverbial—*if*)	Clause
92	Ted's Bed	1, 4	Subordination (adverbial—*when*)	Clause
		2	Preposition embedding *(between)*	Phrase
		3	Coordination *(and)*	Clause
93	Tennis Fan	1, 4	Noun embedding *(tennis)*	Phrase
		2	Subordination (adverbial—*when*)	Clause
		3	Noun embedding *(summer)*	Phrase
94	Ten-Speed Mike	1, 4	Subordination (relative—*who*)	Clause
		2	Verb coordination *(but)*	Phrase
		3	Noun embedding *(ten-speed)*	Phrase
95	Tori's Story	1, 4	Adjective embedding *(gory)*	Phrase
		2	Coordination *(so)*	Clause
		3	Participle embedding *(named)*	Phrase
96	Water Slide Clyde	1, 4	Adjective embedding *(super)*	Phrase
		2	Noun embedding *(water)*	Phrase
		3	Subordination (nominal—*[that]*)	Clause
98	Will's Thrill	1, 4	Subordination (relative—*who*)	Clause
		2	Adjective embedding *(red)*	Phrase
		3	Subordination (adverbial—*when*)	Clause

Level: Difficult (D)

Chant #	Title	Line	Syntactic Structures	Context
2	Bad Days	1, 4	Subordination (adverbial—*when*)	Clause
		2	Verb coordination *(and)*	Phrase
		3	Subordination (relative—*which*)	Clause
7	Cake Hater	1, 4	Coordination *(but)*	Clause
		2	Subordination (nominal—*[that]*)	Clause
		3	Subordination (relative—*which*)	Clause
11	Cool Cat	1, 4	Adjective embedding *(ratty)*	Phrase
		2	Noun coordination *(and + show)*	Phrase
		3	Subordination (adverbial—*while*)	Clause
12	Count to Ten	1, 4	Subordination (adverbial—*when*)	Clause
		2	Adjective embedding *(slow)*	Phrase
		3	Subordination (adverbial—*if*)	Clause
13	Cutoff Jeans	1, 4	Noun coordination *(and + are + their)*	Phrase
		2	Subordination (nominal—*what*)	Clause
		3	Adjective embedding *(cutoff)*	Phrase
16	Don the Dog	1, 4	Subordination (relative—*that*)	Clause
		2	Preposition embedding *(like)*	Phrase
		3	Subordination (relative—*which*)	Clause
21	Fred the Frog	1, 4	Subordination (relative—*that*)	Clause
		2	Preposition embedding *(with)*	Phrase
		3	Subordination (adverbial—*so [that]*)	Clause
22	Frosty Toes	1, 4	Adjective embedding *(bright blue)*	Phrase
		2	Coordination *(and + did)*	Clause
		3	Subordination (adverbial—*when*)	Clause
25	Grandpa's Beard	1, 4	Subordination (adverbial—*because*)	Clause
		2	Adverb embedding *(once a week)*	Phrase
		3	Subordination (adverbial—*while*)	Clause

Level: Difficult (D)—*Continued*

Chant #	Title	Line	Syntactic Structures	Context
26	Green Teeth	1, 4	Subordination (relative—*whose*)	Clause
		2	Infinitive embedding *([in order] to)*	Phrase
		3	Preposition embedding *(on)*	Phrase
31	Hopscotch	1, 4	Infinitive embedding *([in order] to)*	Phrase
		2	Subordination (adverbial—*while*)	Clause
		3	Subordination (adverbial—*if*)	Clause
37	Jogging Dogs	1, 4	Subordination (adverbial—*while*)	Clause
		2	Participle embedding *(creeping)*	Phrase
		3	Adjective embedding *(rotten)*	Phrase
40	Kate the Cat	1, 4	Subordination (relative—*that*)	Clause
		2	Subordination (adverbial—*when*)	Clause
		3	Adjective coordination *(and)*	Phrase
45	Lunch Bunch	1, 4	Adjective embedding *(hungry)*	Phrase
		2	Subordination (adverbial—*when*)	Clause
		3	Subordination (adverbial—*while*)	Clause
46	Math Gal	1, 4	Subordination (relative—*who*)	Clause
		2	Preposition embedding *(along)*	Phrase
		3	Adverb embedding *(while)*	Phrase
47	Milk Shake Cow	1, 4	Subordination (relative—*that*)	Clause
		2	Preposition embedding *(with)*	Phrase
		3	Subordination (adverbial—*when*)	Clause
49	My Friend Paul	1, 4	Subordination (relative—*whose*)	Clause
		2	Coordination *(and)*	Clause
		3	Subordination (relative—*[that]*)	Clause
52	Nice Ice	1, 4	Preposition embedding *(because of)*	Phrase
		2	Adjective coordination *(but)*	Phrase
		3	Subordination (adverbial—*when*)	Clause
58	Pet Pig	1, 4	Noun embedding *(pet)*	Phrase
		2	Subordination (adverbial—*where*)	Clause
		3	Coordination *(but)*	Clause

Level: Difficult (D)—*Continued*

Chant #	Title	Line	Syntactic Structures	Context
61	Reading at Night	1, 4	Adverb embedding *(late at night)*	Phrase
		2	Subordination (relative—*which*)	Clause
		3	Subordination (nominal—*[that]*)	Clause
63	Rhythm, Rhyme, and Rap	1, 4	Noun coordination *(and)*	Phrase
		2	Preposition embedding *(for)*	Phrase
		3	Subordination (adverbial—*while*)	Clause
65	River Raft	1, 4	Subordination (adverbial—*while*)	Clause
		2	Verb coordination *(and)*	Phrase
		3	Noun embedding (river)	Phrase
66	Rob the Robot	1, 4	Appositive noun embedding *(the robot)*	Phrase
		2	Subordination (nominal—*what*)	Clause
		3	Preposition embedding *(on)*	Phrase
67	Rock Climbing	1, 4	Adverb embedding *(slowly)*	Phrase
		2	Participle embedding *(working)*	Phrase
		3	Subordination (adverbial—*as*)	Clause
69	Rose's Clothes	1, 4	Subordination (relative—*who*)	Clause
		2	Subordination (adverbial—*until*)	Clause
		3	Subordination (adverbial—*as*)	Clause
71	Sad Chad	1, 4	Subordination (relative—*who*)	Clause
		2	Subordination (relative—*[that]*)	Clause
		3	Subordination (relative—*which*)	Clause
73	Sharks	1, 4	Coordination *(but)*	Clause
		2	Subordination (relative—*which*)	Clause
		3	Subordination (adverbial—*if*)	Clause
74	Shower Power	1, 4	Subordination (relative—*who*)	Clause
		2	Preposition embedding *(for)*	Phrase
		3	Subordination (relative—*which*)	Clause
75	Shrimp Feast	1, 4	Subordination (adverbial—*when*)	Clause
		2	Subordination (adverbial—*until*)	Clause
		3	Participle embedding *(shrimp-filled)*	Phrase

Level: Difficult (D)—*Continued*

Chant #	Title	Line	Syntactic Structures	Context
77	Skiing Free	1, 4	Subordination (relative—*who*)	Clause
		2	Subordination (adverbial—*though*)	Clause
		3	Subordination (adverbial—*though*)	Clause
82	Snack Attack	1, 4	Subordination (adverbial—*while*)	Clause
		2	Noun coordination *(and + both + get)*	Phrase
		3	Subordination (adverbial—*as*)	Clause
84	Snap-Happy Rap	1, 4	Noun coordination *(and + are)*	Phrase
		2	Noun coordination *(and)*	Phrase
		3	Possessive embedding *(baby's)*	Phrase
90	Surfing	1, 4	Subordination (relative—*that*)	Clause
		2	Verb coordination *(and)*	Phrase
		3	Preposition embedding *(in)*	Phrase
97	Whiz Kid	1, 4	Subordination (relative—*whose*)	Clause
		2	Adjective embedding *(high)*	Phrase
		3	Preposition embedding *(with)*	Phrase
100	Zack and Zaney	1, 4	Subordination (relative—*that*)	Clause
		2	Preposition embedding *(around)*	Phrase
		3	Subordination (adverbial—*as*)	Clause

Rhyme Family	Chant Number and Name
-ace	80: Slow Pace, 100: Zack and Zaney
-ack	3: Bareback Mac, 82: Snack Attack, 83: Snack Packing, 100: Zack and Zaney
-ad	71: Sad Chad, 74: Shower Power, 98: Will's Thrill
-ade	68: Rollerblade Wade
-aft	65: River Raft
-ain	34: Jane's Sprain
-ake	5: Blake Snores, 7: Cake Hater, 9: Chanting
-akes	47: Milk Shake Cow
-ame	56: Pesky Guest, 85: Soccer Game
-amp	76: Skateboard Ramp
-an	42: Kick the Can, 87: Stan the Man, 93: Tennis Fan
-ance	62: Red Ants
-anks	32: Hot Dogs
-ap	63: Rhythm, Rhyme, and Rap, 84: Snap-Happy Rap
-are	58: Pet Pig
-ark	54: Park Shark, 73: Sharks
-ary	86: Spiked Hair
-ash	54: Park Shark
-at	11: Cool Cat, 55: Pat's Cats
-ate	39: Kate Skates, 40: Kate the Cat, 41: Kate's Lunch, 51: Nate the Skater, 76: Skateboard Ramp
-ath	46: Math Gal

Note: Spellings for the rhyme families were based on *The Random House Rhyming Dictionary* (1985), J. Stein (Ed.), New York, Random House. Rhyming words were placed under the most commonly used spelling for a particular sound.

Rhyme Family	Chant Number and Name
-ave	90: Surfing
-awl	49: My Friend Paul, 89: Summertime
-ay	52: Nice Ice, 84: Snap-Happy Rap
-each	20: Flying Free
-eaks	92: Ted's Bed
-eal	44: Lucille Seal
-eam	17: Dream Team
-ean	13: Cutoff Jeans, 26: Green Teeth
-eard	25: Grandpa's Beard
-ease	4: Big Sneeze, 23: Ghost Sounds, 50: Nachos
-eat	27: Halloween Fun, 44: Lucille Seal
-eats	48: Mona the Mouse
-ed	21: Fred the Frog, 82: Snack Attack, 92: Ted's Bed, 98: Will's Thrill
-ee	19: Floyd the Flea, 20: Flying Free, 25: Grandpa's Beard, 26: Green Teeth, 47: Milk Shake Cow, 77: Skiing Free
-eed	61: Reading at Night
-eep	37: Jogging Dogs
-eer	48: Mona the Mouse
-el	81: Smelly Toes
-en	2: Bad Days, 12: Count to Ten, 57: Pet Hen, 85: Soccer Game
-ennis	93: Tennis Fan
-er	55: Pat's Cats
-ert	15: Dog Bath
-erve	33: Irv's Curve
-est	56: Pesky Guest

Rhyme Family	Chant Number and Name
-et	17: Dream Team
-ew	1: Back Flip, 13: Cutoff Jeans, 22: Frosty Toes, 24: Gluey Stew, 37: Jogging Dogs, 69: Rose's Clothes, 77: Skiing Free, 87: Stan the Man, 88: Sugar Blues, 98: Will's Thrill
-ice	51: Nate the Skater, 52: Nice Ice, 64: Rice Pudding
-ick	21: Fred the Frog
-ide	28: Hear the Night, 51: Nate the Skater, 90: Surfing, 96: Water Slide Clyde
-ig	58: Pet Pig
-ike	94: Ten-Speed Mike
-ikes	14: Dirt Bikes
-ild	86: Spiked Hair
-ile	11: Cool Cat
-ill	98: Will's Thrill
-ills	14: Dirt Bikes
-im	38: Jungle Jim, 79: Slim Jim, 91: Swim Song
-ime	43: Lime Slime
-imp	75: Shrimp Feast
-in	2: Bad Days
-ine	9: Chanting, 29: Hiking
-ip	1: Back Flip, 2: Bad Days, 77: Skiing Free
-ipt	34: Jane's Sprain
-is	16: Don the Dog, 21: Fred the Frog, 70: Rude Dude, 71: Sad Chad, 97: Whiz Kid
-itches	19: Floyd the Flea
-ite	18: Fall Colors, 28: Hear the Night, 73: Sharks
-it	53: Numb Thumb

Rhyme Family	Chant Number and Name
-ow	9: Chanting, 12: Count to Ten, 21: Fred the Frog, 26: Green Teeth, 31: Hopscotch, 33: Irv's Curve, 47: Milk Shake Cow, 49: My Friend Paul, 51: Nate the Skater, 57: Pet Hen, 61: Reading at Night, 64: Rice Pudding, 77: Skiing Free, 80: Slow Pace, 81: Smelly Toes, 83: Snack Packing, 89: Summertime, 95: Tori's Story, 97: Whiz Kid
-owl	15: Dog Bath, 27: Halloween Fun
-owls	40: Kate the Cat
-uck	10: Chuck's Truck
-ude	59: Popcorn, 70: Rude Dude
-udge	23: Ghost Sounds
-ugs	8: Camping
-um	53: Numb Thumb
-un	87: Stan the Man
-unch	45: Lunch Bunch, 59: Popcorn
-unk	78: Skunk Trunk
-urps	70: Rude Dude
-urst	70: Rude Dude
-y	7: Cake Hater, 20: Flying Free, 31: Hopscotch, 53: Numb Thumb, 61: Reading at Night, 62: Red Ants, 78: Skunk Trunk, 81: Smelly Toes, 97: Whiz Kid

Phrase Structure

Difficulty Rating Scale: E = Easy; M = Moderate; D = Difficult
* Indicates chants where the syntactic structure occurs more than once
** SV = subject/verb agreement

Coordination

Syntactic Structure	Difficulty Level	Chant Number
Adjective		
and	E	53
	M	72, 79*, 91
	D	40
but	D	52
or	E	59
Noun		
and	E	33*, 60*, 62
	M	14, 27, 29*, 36, 68*
	D	63*, 84
and + SV**	M	15*, 51, 57*
	D	11, 13*, 82, 84*
but	E	80
or	E	60
	M	27*
Verb		
and	E	3, 9, 33, 53
	M	4, 15, 17, 34, 36, 87, 88, 91*
	D	2, 65, 90
but	E	80*
	M	87, 94
or	E	99
	M	1,
then	M	39*, 70, 85

Embedding

Syntactic Structure	Difficulty Level	Chant Number
Adjective	E	54, 59*, 80
	M	1*, 10, 18, 20, 29, 30, 32*, 35*, 57, 70, 72, 86*, 88*, 95*, 96*, 98
	D	11*, 12, 13, 22*, 37, 45*, 97
Adverb		
-ly	D	67*
phrase	E	9*, 89*
	M	4, 8, 34, 43
	D	25, 46, 61*
Appositive		
noun	M	10*
	D	66*
adjective	M	30
Gerund	M	18, 76*
Infinitive	M	44, 79
	D	26, 31*
Noun	E	3, 62*, 83*
	M	8, 10, 14, 30*, 76, 85*, 93*, 94, 96
	D	58*, 65
Participle	E	33
	M	42, 95
	D	37, 67, 75

Phrase Structure: Embedding—*Continued*

Syntactic Structure	Difficulty Level	Chant Number	Syntactic Structure	Difficulty Level	Chant Number
Possessive	M	5, 38*	inside	M	78*, 79
	D	84	like	E	55
				M	44*, 50, 56
Preposition				D	16
along	D	46	of	M	6
around	D	100	off	M	35
at	E	54*	on	M	32, 51*
	M	20*		D	26, 66
because of	M	8*	till	E	54
	D	52*	to	E	3*
behind	M	4*	until	M	5*
beneath	M	38	up	M	23
between	M	92	upon	M	19
beyond	M	20	with	M	5, 36*, 41, 50*
by	M	51		D	21, 47, 97
for	M	6, 19, 78	without	M	48
	D	63, 74			
from	M	56			
from off	M	41*			
in	E	62, 83*			
	M	14*, 23*, 28, 34*			
	D	90			

Clause Structure

Difficulty Rating Scale: E = Easy; M = Moderate; D = Difficult

* Indicates chants where the syntactic structure occurs more than once

** SV = subject/verb agreement

Coordination

Syntactic Structure	Difficulty Level	Chant Number
and	E	24*, 55*, 64*, 81*, 89, 99*
	M	6*, 15, 28*, 32, 39, 42, 76, 92
	D	22, 49

Syntactic Structure	Difficulty Level	Chant Number
but	M	29, 39, 78
	D	7*, 58, 73*
or	E	99
	M	44
so	E	89
	M	95

Subordination

Syntactic Structure	Difficulty Level	Chant Number
Adverbial		
after	M	17
as	M	18*, 23, 28
	D	67, 69, 82, 100
because	M	72*
	D	25*
if	M	1, 35, 42*, 88, 91
	D	12, 31, 73
so [that]	E	81*
	D	21
though	D	77*
until	D	69, 75
when	E	9, 60
	M	43*, 48, 85, 92*, 93, 98
	D	2*, 12*, 22, 40, 45, 47, 52, 75*
where	D	58
while	M	86
	D	11, 25, 31, 37*, 45, 63, 65*, 82*

Syntactic Structure	Difficulty Level	Chant Number
Nominal		
that	M	41, 56*, 68
[that]	M	50, 96
	D	7, 61
what	D	13, 66
Relative		
that	E	24*, 53*
	M	17*, 38, 43, 48*, 57
	D	16*, 21*, 40*, 47*, 90*, 100*
[that]	M	19*, 27
	D	49, 71
which	D	2, 7, 16, 61, 71, 73, 74
who	M	70*, 87*, 94*, 98*
	D	46*, 69*, 71*, 74*, 77*
whose	D	26*, 49*, 97*